D0409958

INTRODUCING THE EARTH
Geology, Environment, and Man

OTHER BOOKS BY
WILLIAM H. MATTHEWS III

FOSSILS: AN INTRODUCTION TO PREHISTORIC LIFE
WONDERS OF THE DINOSAUR WORLD
EXPLORING THE WORLD OF FOSSILS
TEXAS FOSSILS: AN AMATEUR COLLECTOR'S HANDBOOK
GEOLOGY MADE SIMPLE
A GUIDE TO THE NATIONAL PARKS:
THEIR GEOLOGY AND LANDSCAPES
THE STORY OF THE EARTH
WONDERS OF FOSSILS
THE STORY OF VOLCANOES AND EARTHQUAKES
SCIENCE PROBES THE EARTH: NEW FRONTIERS OF GEOLOGY
THE FIRST BOOK OF SOILS
THE FIRST BOOK OF THE EARTH'S CRUST
INVITATION TO GEOLOGY: THE EARTH THROUGH TIME AND SPACE

INTRODUCING THE EARTH

Geology, Environment, and Man

William H. Matthews III

ILLUSTRATED WITH PHOTOGRAPHS AND DIAGRAMS

DODD, MEAD & COMPANY
New York

In memory of my grandparents,
ANNE ELIZABETH and WILLIAM HENRY MATTHEWS

PREFACE

Earth is our home and man has relied on this planet since prehistoric time. Why, then, should anyone need an "introduction" to the earth? The earth—like air, water, and other commonplace objects—is all too often taken for granted. In fact, we commonly know more about our automobiles and television sets than we know about the earth beneath our very feet.

This book will introduce you to planet Earth and its environment in space. It will attempt to answer questions that have puzzled man for thousands of years: Where did Earth come from? How old is it? What causes volcanoes, earthquakes, and landslides? What is the earth made of? And how and by what means has Earth changed during its 4½-billion-year-old-history? Equally important, what is the future of our fragile planet with its load of plants and animals? And what can the geologist do to conserve our priceless mineral resources and preserve the environment?

You will be richer for having been introduced to the earth. Even a passing acquaintance with earth science can greatly enhance your appreciation for our earthly home. It will enable you to see more of the earth around you. And—hopefully—you will understand more of what you see.

A number of people have helped to make this book possible and I would like to thank the following: Mrs. Joe Ann Daly, Dodd, Mead & Company, made numerous helpful suggestions; Mr. Wil Dooley of the United States Geological Survey provided many of the illustrations; and the manuscript was typed by Susan Gribnau and Margaret Crabtree. Most of all I thank my wife, Jennie. She critically read and edited the entire manuscript, took many of the photographs, and prepared the index. But most of all, she supplied the encouragement and understanding that enabled me to write the book.

WILLIAM H. MATTHEWS III
Beaumont, Texas

CONTENTS

CONTENTS

INTRODUCING THE EARTH
Geology, Environment, and Man

This photograph of "our amazing Earth" was taken from about 98,000 nautical miles above the earth by Apollo 11 astronauts. It reveals most of Africa and portions of Asia and Europe.

Chapter 1

OUR AMAZING EARTH

A sudden spasm in the earth and thousands of Californians literally roll out of their beds. In southern Italy, Mount Etna rouses from a smouldering nap and villagers pray that their favorite saints will stem the fiery tide of lava. A mountainside tears loose in Peru—when the dust settles an entire village has disappeared. Hardly a week passes without a similar report on Earth's seemingly "unruly" behavior. The all-too-familiar scenes of tongues of lava and collapsed houses are well known to most of us, for such natural disasters are certainly dramatic and news-worthy events. They are also of significance to man—especially to those who were bounced out of bed, burned by lava, or buried under tons of rocks.

But there are two sides to every story, and fortunately the good points of our amazing planet far outweigh its weaknesses. What is so amazing about a ball of rock, that is almost three-fourths covered by water, and completely enclosed in a shell of air? For one thing—and this is enough—Earth is our home. Earth's solid part, the "ball of rock," is called the *lithosphere*. The rocks of the lithosphere provide a solid foundation upon which to live. They also provide man with much-needed natural resources. The *hydrosphere*, a widespread sheet of water that covers almost 71 per cent of the earth's surface, is so basic that life could not exist without it. We breath air from the *atmosphere*, the thick envelope of gas that completely surrounds the earth. These three zones of matter—lithosphere, hydrosphere, and atmosphere—make possible the existence of a fourth zone called the *biosphere*. This is literally the "sphere of life," for it is composed of the earth's living plants and animals. As we shall see later, each of these spheres plays a vital role in the composition of the earth and the various natural processes at work on it.

We generally find comfort in the fact that the earth never seems to change. We speak of the good "solid earth" or *terra firma*. In fact, Earth has always been considered the ultimate symbol of strength and stability. But though our planet may appear to be ageless and eternal, it is neither. Earthquakes, volcanic eruptions, and landslides occur periodically and they are dramatic evidence of the natural and inevitable change in our restless planet. Much more common—and important—are the less dramatic changes on the earth's surface: sediments accumulating on the ocean floor; mountains being slowly eroded away; barren rock breaking down to form fertile soil. In short, the materials and processes of the earth work for man in many ways and literally make possible the habitable Earth.

Chapter 2

THE EARTH IN TIME
AND SPACE

Have you ever looked at the star-filled sky on a dark, clear night and wondered what was up "there?" And did you stop to think how the sun, the moon, and our own planet Earth might fit into that heavenly scene? If such questions *did* cross your mind, you were in very good company, for scientists have puzzled over the mysteries of the universe for more than two hundred years.

Fortunately, they have not wondered in vain, for much has been learned. Astronomers have long since assigned Earth to its own little niche in the universe and its vital statistics are quite well known. And—thanks to the breathtaking photographs taken from space and eyewitness reports by astronauts—we now have a totally new image of the billions-of-years-old planet that we call home.

The view from space is exciting. It is also somewhat frightening. As we see this fragile globe suspended in space, we realize that Earth and its precious cargo of life occupies but a minute part of an incredibly vast universe. It is also obvious that man's environment is extremely restricted. For now, at least, there is really no other place to go. This rather grim perspective—along with growing problems of pollution and overpopulation—has caused some well-founded concerns about the future of our en-

Ancient Egyptians thought of the "heavens" as a bent-over goddess supported by the god of the atmosphere.

vironment. It has also spawned increasing numbers of predictions as to the "end of the world."

Although concerned about the future of the earth and our environment, astronomers and geologists are also interested in the history of our planet. As these scientists study Earth's cloud-shrouded outline, many questions come to mind. But the question that most frequently arises is one that has puzzled man since the dawn of history: Where did Earth come from and what is its relation to the other bodies in space?

In ancient times this question was answered in the light of superstition and legend. The Egyptians saw the earth as a reclining god covered with plants. To the Babylonians it was a hollow mountain surrounded and supported by the sea. Even now—in this enlightened Age of Space—the mystery remains largely unsolved. But thanks to *cosmogonists* (scientists concerned with the origin of stars and planets) we do have some "educated guesses" to explain Earth's creation. Yet none of these hypotheses answer all of our questions about the earth's beginnings, and serious objections have been raised against each of them.

EARTH'S PLACE IN THE UNIVERSE

Although it is the geologist who has revealed most of our planet's secrets, astronomers have done much to help the earth scientist understand more clearly the relation of Earth to its companions in space. Astronomers have long known that the earth belongs to a small group of heavenly bodies called the *solar system*. The solar system, in turn, is part of a much larger group called the Milky Way galaxy. A great disc-shaped mass containing about 100 billion stars, the Milky Way is but one of perhaps a billion galaxies in our universe.

Although the Milky Way is not an exceptionally large galaxy, its size still boggles the mind. Because of the vastness of the universe, the astronomer measures distance in units called *light-years*. Each light-year represents the distance that light travels in one year at the speed of 186,234 miles per second. Or, stated in the terms of distance, one light-year is equal to almost six *trillion* miles! To appreciate better the speed of light, let us consider what could happen if we should send a beam of light across the United States from the Atlantic to the Pacific coast—a distance of 3000 miles. Amazingly enough, that beam of light would complete thirty-one round trips in only *one* second! With this understanding of the great distance involved in a light-year, we can appreciate more fully the remoteness of space. We can also better visualize the immensity of the Milky Way galaxy, which measures some 100,000 light-years in diameter and is about 25,000 light-years thick.

One does not have to be an astronomer to locate the Milky Way, for it appears as a bright pathway splashed against the evening sky. This soft milky streak is especially noticeable on a clear but moonless night and is produced by the glow of some

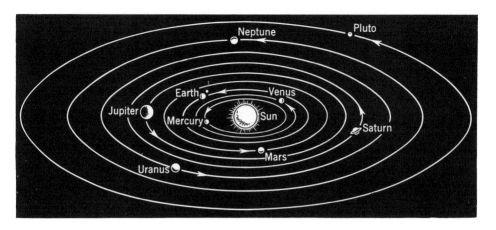

Planets of our solar system and their paths around the sun.

100 billion stars. One of these stars—the *sun*—is of great importance to man. The sun is not only the center of our solar system, it makes life possible on Earth and provides most of the continuing energy supply at the earth's surface.

Speeding endlessly around the sun are the nine planets of our solar system. Mercury is closest to the sun, followed by Venus, Earth, and Mars. Next come Jupiter, Saturn, Uranus, and Neptune. And last—as well as least—is little Pluto. Other members of the sun's "family" include the *asteroids*, planet-like bodies located in a belt between the orbits of Mars and Jupiter. Present also are comets, meteors, and natural satellites, or moons. The moons revolve around their respective planets much as the planets revolve around the sun. The satellites are not evenly distributed among the planets, for Mercury, Venus, and Pluto have no known moons. Jupiter, on the other hand, has twelve.

IN THE BEGINNING

Have Earth, our solar system, and the universe always been here? How did they have their beginnings? Because Earth is but one rather small part of the solar system, any attempt to explain its creation must also account for the origin of the entire system.

One of the earliest attempts to account for the planets was made more than two hundred years ago by the Comte de Buffon. This distinguished French scholar proposed that the planets had been formed as the result of a collision between the sun and a large mass of celestial matter. The impact of this stellar collision dislodged huge blobs of matter that later formed the planets. Although Buffon supported this idea by performing timed experiments on balls of metal and rock, he lacked sufficient information to prove his theory. He did, however, correctly assume the earth to be much older than originally believed. He suggested, moreover, that the six days of creation may have been six long epochs of time.

In 1755, a German philosopher named Immanuel Kant stated that the solar system originated from a spinning gaseous mass called a *nebula*. Developed more fully in 1796 by French mathematician Pierre Laplace, the *nebular hypothesis* assumes the presence of a nebula that is slowly rotating through space. The nebula gradually cooled and became smaller and this shrinkage

Early nebular theories to explain the origin of the solar system suggest that a large, slowly rotating cloud of dust and gas gradually contracted and flattened. Rings of the material were left behind, and the planets condensed from these.

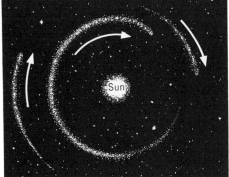

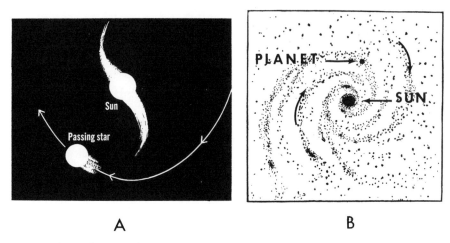

A   B

According to the planetesimal hypothesis, a passing star pulled large masses of gas from the sun which later condensed to form the planets (A). (B) represents a stage in solar system development when planetesimals are accumulating around the larger nuclei. Some of these have attained the size of planets.

caused it to spin more rapidly. The nebula eventually rotated so fast that rings of gas were thrown off. Ten rings were produced in this way and nine of them condensed to become the planets. The other ring broke into smaller masses that formed the asteroids. The remaining central nebular mass became the sun.

In 1900, two University of Chicago professors, Forest R. Moulton, an astronomer, and Thomas C. Chamberlin, a geologist, came forth with the *planetesimal hypothesis*. They assumed that the sun was originally a star without planets. In the distant past, another star passed very close to the sun. This "near miss" produced a gravitational force strong enough to tear large masses of solar matter from opposite sides of the sun. This detached solar material condensed to form solid particles called *planetesimals* and these formed the nucleus of each planet. In their sweep around the sun, the planets steadily accumulate additional planetesimal matter and eventually grew to their present size.

The *gaseous tidal hypothesis* was proposed in 1918 by Sir James Jeans, a physicist, and Sir Harold Jeffreys, an astronomer. It also assumes a near-collision of an original planetless sun with another star. Tidal action of the intruder star ripped a threadlike mass of gaseous matter from the sun. This cigar-shaped filament later broke into smaller blobs of gas and these eventually condensed to form the planets of our solar system.

These early theories were at least a beginning. But as more was learned about the universe all of these ideas were eventually discredited. Indeed, for many years it seemed as if science was actually making progress toward proving that the solar system could *not* have been formed!

A NEW LOOK AT AN OLD IDEA

How do today's astronomers account for the solar system? Oddly enough, cosmogonists have retuned to the idea that the sun and planets originated from a cloud of gas and dust. But where earlier nebular theories centered around the physical behavior of the sun's family, the modern approach pays special attention to the chemical composition of the solar system.

Astronomers have discovered many large clouds of dust and gas between the stars in our galaxy. More important, some of these nebulae are condensing to form stars. Nebulae that are not rotating condense to form single stars without planets. But rapidly rotating nebulae develop great "whirlpools" (or eddies) that may break into two or more parts. Fragments of these "whirlpools" may form double—or even triple—stars.

These observations led to the *dust cloud* or *protoplanet hypothesis* that was first suggested in 1944 by Carl F. von Weizsacker (a German astrophysicist) and later modified by Gerard P. Kuiper, an American astronomer. This theory assumes an interstellar cloud of dust and gas spinning slowly through space. Gradually, the center of the nebula condensed to form a large

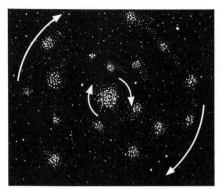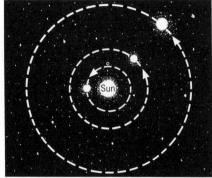

A more recent neubular theory assumes that large condensations called "protoplanets" condensed from the flattened, rotating neubula around the central sun.

mass—a *protosun* from which our sun evolved. The remaining "dust cloud" flattened into a thin disc around the newborn star and rotation of the disc caused whirlpool-like vortexes to form in the cloud. Then, by means of gravitational attraction, each swirl collected the material around it, thereby creating a *protoplanet*. Nine protoplanets—one for each planet in the solar system—are thought to have been formed.

When did this happen and how long did it take? The oldest rocks on Earth suggest that our planet is about 4½ billion years old. Cosmogonists add another billion years, for they assume it took that long for the nebular material to reach its original earthly state.

Scientists generally accept the protoplanet hypothesis because it explains more things better than any other theory. Does this mean that we have the "final answer?" Far from it. Although admittedly based on firmer ground than earlier theories, this hypothesis is far from complete and sure to be revised as we learn more about the universe. In short, man continues to ask—as he has for thousands of years—where, when, and how did Earth come to be?

Chapter 3

EARTH AS A PLANET

Despite the confusion and mystery surrounding the origin of the earth, we do know a great deal about its physical characteristics. Indeed, man has made rather accurate estimates about the size and shape of the earth for more than two thousand years.

ROUND, OUT-OF-ROUND, OR PEAR-SHAPED?

In your schoolroom, or perhaps on your desk at home, there may be a globe which shows certain features of the earth. But although this ball-shaped model shows the earth to be spherical or globe-shaped, Earth is more properly described as an *oblate spheroid*. This means that our globe is really not a globe at all, for instead of being a perfect sphere, Earth is somewhat flattened at the poles. This polar flattening, in turn, produces a slight bulge at the earth's equator.

Why has Earth assumed this particular form? Why is it not in the shape of a square, a cone, or a banana? The more-or-less spherical shape of the earth is due to the force of *gravity*. This force—which steadily pulls toward the center of the earth—tends to keep all parts of Earth's surface at an equal distance from its center. This does not mean, of course, that the surface of the earth is perfectly smooth. We know that there are relatively minor irregularities such as mountain chains and deep ocean basins. But these features are hardly noticeable on a global scale and have little effect on the pressure balance within the earth.

You may be wondering about the cause of the polar flattening and equatorial bulge that cause our planet to be slightly out-of-round. This distortion is produced by *centrifugal force*. This apparent outward force or centrifugal effect is developed as the earth spins on its axis. Centrifugal force, like the force of gravity, is in continual operation around us. An automobile driving through a puddle of water will throw water on the windshield of the car behind it. As the wheel spins, most of the water flies off the wheel and away from it. By the same token, our rapidly rotating earth develops a strong centrifugal force at the equator. This causes the earth's surface to be forced away from its center, thereby producing the bulge.

Why are objects on the earth's equatorial surface not spun off into space? Luckily, the inward pull of the force of gravity tends to counteract the outward pull of the centrifugal effect.

Within recent years measurements made from earth-orbiting satellites have shown yet another "deformity" on our not-so-round planet. Curiously enough, the equatorial bulge is actually about twenty-five feet south of the exact middle of the earth. In other words, the earth is a bit fatter in the Southern Hemisphere than it is in the Northern Hemisphere, or "top half." Unfortunately, this slightly off-center bulge has led a few observers to refer to the earth as being "pear-shaped."

THE SIZE OF THE EARTH

An astronaut's view of Earth reveals that our planet is not as large as we might like to think. In fact, compared to most of her sister planets, the sun, and other stars, Earth is a relatively small celestial body. It is, nonetheless, a quite sizable object, for it has a circumference of about 24,860 miles. Because of its shape, the diameter of the earth varies according to where it is measured. If the measurement is made at sea level from the North Pole through the earth's center to the South Pole we arrive at a figure of slightly less than 7900 miles. If a similar measurement is made through the earth in its equatorial plane, its diameter increases by 26.8 miles. The difference is due, of course, to the faint bulge produced by the rotation of the plant.

As might be expected, an object of such great size is also likely to be quite heavy. Thanks to the work of a number of early scientists, we have long known that Earth has a mass (or "weight") of some 6595 million million million tons!

EARTH—PLANET ON THE MOVE

Although astronauts have described the earth as appearing to be "suspended" or "dangling" in space, our dynamic planet is far from motionless. On the contrary, this apparently immobile planet is spinning, orbiting, and hurtling through space at astonishing speeds. In fact, it even has a bit of a wobble.

Most of us know that the earth rotates (or spins like a top) and that it revolves around the sun. These two motions have a very important effect on man's environment. They are largely responsible for day and night, the rise and fall of the tides, the seasons, and weather and climate.

Rotation occurs as Earth spins on an imaginary *axis* which is the shortest diameter connecting the poles. Completing one rotation every twenty-four hours, the earth spins from west to east and this gives us our alternating periods of daylight and darkness.

You can produce your own "night" and "day" by shining a flashlight on a globe in a darkened room. Turn the globe very slowly and notice how the different oceans and continents gradually move into the shadows. This explains better than words why at any given time it is daylight on the half of the earth that is facing the sun. The other half of the world is experiencing the darkness of night.

How fast does Earth spin on its axis? Its greatest velocity (speed) of rotation is at the equator. According to one method

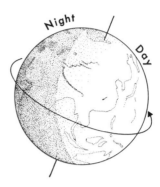

Night and day are the result of the earth's twenty-four-hour period of rotation.

of calculating the velocity of rotation, a man standing at the equator is moving at about 1040 miles per hour! On the other hand, a person located exactly at the earth's pole would not move in a circle. He would simply spin around once every twenty-four hours. Despite this motion, neither of the above men would have the slightest feeling of movement. This is because all of their surroundings would be moving along with them and there would be no sensation of motion.

Because Earth's axis is inclined, the sun's rays reach the Northern Hemisphere most directly during part of its orbit around the sun, thus producing summer. During other parts of the revolution, they reach the Southern Hemisphere most directly, causing winter. At intermediate periods, the rays strike most directly near the equator, resulting in fall and spring.

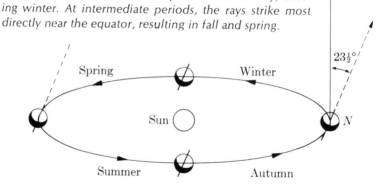

Like its rotation, the revolution of the earth follows a very definite and dependable path or orbit. Although seemingly motionless, Earth is actually whirling around the sun at an average speed of about 60,000 miles per hour. Even at this incredible speed it takes the earth 365 ¼ days (one solar year) to complete its journey around our parent star. This is not surprising when we consider that one trip around the orbit covers 683,942,855 miles.

The earth's orbit is much like that of a space vehicle or man-made satellite, because it follows an elliptical path. This means that the orbit is not quite circular; hence, the earth does not always remain the same distance from the sun. Its average distance from the sun is approximately 93 million miles, but is farthest from the sun in July and closest in January.

What about Earth's wobble? Like a spinning top, the axis of the earth wobbles, or *precesses*, as it spins. This happens because the earth's axis is inclined at an angle of 23½ degrees. This axial tilt causes the sun and moon to exert changing gravitational attractions on the earth, thus causing the gyrational motion called *precession*. Luckily, this wobbling motion is so slow that it takes 26,000 years to complete a single wobble.

But our spinning, orbiting, wobbling earth is moving in yet another way. Along with its companions in the solar system, Earth is rushing through space at a speed of about twelve miles per second. Our destination? No one knows exactly *where* we are going, but we are heading in the general direction of a star known as Vega. A large star in the constellation of Lyra, Vega is the second brightest star visible in northern latitudes.

Clearly, Earth is not the stationary and static planet that it might appear to be. It is also not surprising that the earth has been referred to as a "spaceship." We should be glad that our planet is on the move, for its various motions play an important role in our lives.

Chapter 4

DOWN TO EARTH—
A CLOSER LOOK

Thanks to the wonders of television and the wizardry of space technology, most of us have been treated to an astronaut's view of the earth. But more importantly, information gathered by astronomers and space scientists has more clearly outlined Earth's setting in the Universe. Their studies are also helping us to understand better the origin of the earth and its relation to our moon and the other members of the solar system. This is good, for we should know as much about our planet as possible. Earth's size and shape, its various movements, and its position in the solar system have—either directly or indirectly—considerable effect on man.

The view of the earth in space is most intriguing. But to really understand our planet, we must come down to Earth for a closer look at this ancient ball of air, water, land, and life.

OUR THIN SHELL OF AIR

Pictures of the earth in space are familiar to us all. Countless photographs have been taken by orbiting space vehicles and these have been snapped from a variety of angles and altitudes. Even so, virtually all of these photographs have one thing in common: clouds. These ever-present clouds represent the visible portion of

The atmosphere is a vital part of our planet. Here, a tethered balloon supports a meteorological instrument above the oceanographic ship, Discoverer.

the atmosphere—a life-giving shell of air that completely surrounds the earth.

Why consider the atmosphere in a book about the earth? Primarily because it is as much a part of our planet as the ground that we stand on or the water that we drink. As mentioned earlier, the atmosphere represents the gaseous matter of the earth, just as the hydrosphere typifies Earth's waters or liquid matter. Likewise, the solid matter of the earth is represented by the rocks, soils, and minerals of the lithosphere. In addition, the atmosphere is involved in a number of processes that affect both the water and the land.

Perhaps more important, Earth's zone of life—the biosphere—would probably not exist without this protective blanket of air. The atmosphere's oxygen and nitrogen are indispensable to life and it also screens out the deadly ultraviolet and X-rays produced by the sun.

The outermost and least dense of Earth's zones of matter, the atmosphere, consists of approximately 78 per cent nitrogen and 21 per cent oxygen. Also present are tiny amounts of carbon dioxide, water vapor, and certain other gases. Although minute traces of atmospheric gases may be found as much as 6000 miles above sea level, about one-half of the entire atmosphere is located between the earth's surface and 18,000 feet (3½ miles). The remaining half lies between an altitude of 3½ miles and 600 miles or more.

Meteorologists, scientists who study the atmosphere, have learned that the atmosphere can be divided into several layers. The zone closest to the surface of the land and sea extends upward for some eight or ten miles. This layer is vital to life, for it provides the air that we breathe. Here, too, is the weather-making part of the atmosphere. Weather not only affects man, it has a profound effect on the rocks and waters of the earth.

Perhaps you have heard the atmosphere called an "ocean of air." Unfortunately, this comparison is somewhat misleading, for unlike Earth's ocean of water, the air "ocean" does not have a well-defined surface. Instead, its upper part fades gradually into the outer reaches of space. These two "oceans" do, however, have some significant features in common. The lithosphere forms the bottom of both the liquid ocean and the gaseous atmosphere, for their undersurfaces are in contact with the earth's crust. Both of these "oceans" are in constant motion, and their movements or circulation produce forces that act upon Earth's surface. We know these motions as ocean waves and currents, wind, as well as rain, snow, and other types of precipitation. Finally, both air and water are essential to support the life of the biosphere.

THE WATER PLANET?

Even a glance at a model of the globe or a world map reveals striking divisions of the land and water. The land, in the form of continents or islands, represents that part of the lithosphere that is not covered by the hydrosphere. Equally striking are the relative amounts of land and water, for 70.8 per cent of the face of the earth is covered by a world-wide sea. Averaging two miles in depth, this far-flung body of water covers more than 140 million square miles. How much water is contained in this vast sea? The ocean basins hold about 300 billion cubic miles of sea water. To better appreciate this tremendous amount of water, look at it this way. If our planet were perfectly smooth—no islands, continents, or mountains—there would be no dry land. Instead, the waters of the ocean would cover the entire earth to a depth of about two miles! Interestingly enough, most of this sea water is concentrated south of the equator, for some 81 per cent of the Southern Hemisphere is flooded by the sea.

Like the atmosphere, the sea is ever-moving and constantly changing. Its tides, currents, and restless waves affect man and his environment in many ways. It is also the source of much food, and salt and other mineral resources which have been extracted from its waters.

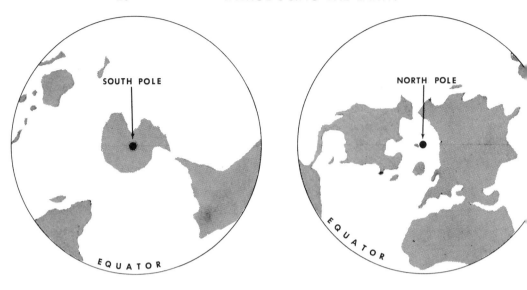

Most of the earth's waters are located in the Southern Hemisphere.

Oceanographers have learned much about the oceans, but many mysteries remain. Consider, for example, the fact that man has traveled a quarter of a million miles to sample and study the surface of the moon. Yet the deep ocean trenches—some seven miles beneath the sea—have not yet been explored.

Although 95 per cent of Earth's water is in the sea, the hydrosphere also includes the water locked up in the ice of glaciers, and the ground water within the earth. Rivers, lakes, ponds, and other bodies of water make up the balance of Earth's valuable supply of fresh water.

Astronomers believe that Earth has more water than any of the other planets in our solar system. If there should be no life on the other eight planets, this lack of sufficient water might be partially responsible.

The earth's waters are not only essential to life, they enter into a number of earth processes. Streams of running water are actively engaged in eroding, transporting, and depositing earth materials. In addition, the sea continually gnaws at the land, wearing it away and depositing rock fragments on the ocean floor. And beneath the earth's surface, ground water dissolves minerals from the subsurface formations, leaving cavities that may become caves. It is generally agreed that water—ably assisted by atmospheric weathering—has been the major force creating the earth's landscapes.

THE SOLID EARTH

As much as we rely upon the gaseous and liquid parts of the earth, it is the solid part—the lithosphere—that provides the firm foundation upon which we live. When we think of a solid we usually think of rocks, for we commonly say that some object is as "solid as a rock."

Derived from the Greek words *lithos*, meaning rock, and *sphaira* (a ball), the term lithosphere graphically describes the "ball of rock" that was mentioned earlier. It is the lithosphere that is of greatest importance to the geologist or earth scientist, for its rocks and minerals yield vital information about the origin and composition of our planet. These solid earth materials also make up the landmasses and ocean basins which are the major surface features of the earth.

There are many processes operating within and on the surface of the "rock-sphere." The earthquakes, volcanoes, and landslides noted earlier are associated with it, as are the less dramatic processes of weathering and erosion.

The lithosphere consists of three basic types of rock: *igneous*, *sedimentary*, and *metamorphic*. Originally in a molten condition, the igneous rocks have since cooled to produce rocks such as granite and lava. Most sedimentary rocks have formed from sediments consisting of the fragments of pre-existing rocks that were deposited by water, wind, or glacial ice. However, some sedimentary rocks have been created through the action of plants and animals as well as chemical reactions. Such common rocks as sandstone, clay, coal, and limestone are typical sedimentary rocks. The metamorphic rocks are quite different. They consist of rocks that were originally igneous or of sedimentary origin. They have been altered—as a result of great physical and chemical change—into a totally different type of rock. Marble, originally limestone, is a familiar example of a metamorphic rock.

Most of what we know about the lithosphere has been learned through the study of surface rocks. However, much has been learned by studying once-deeply buried rocks that are now exposed on the surface. Ancient rocks of this kind can be seen in deeply eroded areas such as the Grand Canyon of the Colorado River. Others have been brought to the earth's surface by great uplifts such as mountain-building or earthquake movements. The deeper part of the lithosphere is not so well known. Yet, as we

The summit of Colorado's 14,110-foot Pikes Peak is composed of igneous rock. Sedimentary rocks can be seen in the foreground. Such rocks make up a large part of the lithosphere.

Colorado Visitors Bureau

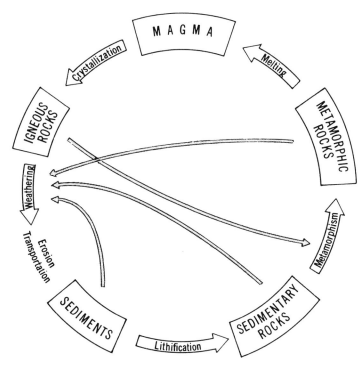

The rock cycle, if uninterrupted, will continue completely around the outer margin of the diagram. However, as shown by the arrows, the cycle may be interrupted or "short-circuited" at various points in its course.

shall soon see, geologists have learned a great deal about the inner parts of the earth.

THE REALM OF LIFE

Can you imagine a world without plants and animals? Life—like air, water, and land—is all around us. So much so, in fact, that it is all too often taken for granted. But the biosphere has not always been present. Although Earth is at least 4½ billion years old, the earliest life forms did not appear until about one billion years later. It appears that life could not originate and develop until the lithosphere, atmosphere, and hydrosphere had attained their "just-right" composition and balance.

The modern world contains an incredibly large number and variety of organisms. There are forests, prairies, and deserts; coral reefs, bays, and lagoons—each populated by countless species of plants and animals. These life forms range in size from the submicroscopic organisms in the air we breathe to the giant sequoia trees of California. This teeming horde of organisms has adapted to almost any environment on earth. Some species live in hot springs or burning desert sands; others thrive in polar climates or on glacial ice. Organisms have been photographed miles below sea level on the ocean floor. They have also been found in the upper part of the atmosphere more than ten miles above Earth's surface. Simple life forms have even been found in water taken from oil wells more than a mile inside the earth.

What does geology, the study of the earth, have to do with the biosphere and the study of life? The sphere of life is no less important than Earth's physical zones. Plants and animals are in continual interaction with the other spheres of the earth and they are involved in a number of important earth processes. Consider such valuable economic products as coal and petroleum: both have been formed from the remains of prehistoric organisms. Many rocks, especially some limestones, are also of organic origin. In addition, there are bacteria that play a key role in the development of certain types of iron ore, and perhaps in the formation of petroleum.

Our interest in the biosphere reaches far back into the past. Geologists study the record of prehistoric life as revealed by fossils in an attempt to learn more about the history of the earth. They have also used these millions-of-years-old plant and animal remains to trace the development of life on Earth.

The spheres of the earth are rather clearly defined and each has its own special role in the over-all composition of the planet. However, the boundaries between them are not always as distinct. Instead, they are continually intermingling as air touches

Once part of the biosphere, these fossils are examples of the way in which plants and animals may be incorporated into the lithosphere.

rock, rock comes in contact with water, water mixes with air. There is constant interaction between Earth's spheres of matter, and important changes occur at the *interface*, or boundary, between them. These changes have been taking place for billions of years and will probably continue for billions more.

With the exception of occasional natural upsets such as hurricanes, floods, earthquakes, and plagues, Nature has a way of keeping the interaction between the spheres in balance. However, within recent years there has been considerable imbalance between the biosphere and Earth's zones of physical matter. This largely man-made upset has resulted in excessive pollution of our air, land, and water.

Earth scientists are quite interested in the interaction of these two zones. They are particularly concerned about the changes that occur at the various interfaces, or boundaries, between them. These changes, many of which are familiar to us all, have done much to shape our physical environment and influence our lives.

Chapter 5

GEOLOGY—
THE KEY TO EARTH'S SECRETS

Casting a cautious glance at the still-twirling rotor blades, the khaki-clad young man leaped from the helicopter and scurried across the deck. Fifty feet beneath him the restless waters of the Gulf of Mexico ceaselessly pounded the massive steel pillars that supported the drilling rig. And from behind came the steady drone of powerful diesel engines spinning the bit attached to the two-mile string of drill pipe that was probing the sediments beneath the water.

But if the young man was aware of the noise and the air of expectation that was obvious among the drilling crew, he certainly did not show it. "May I have the last sample, please?" he asked as he removed a microscope from the case that he had brought with him. Quickly opening the small cloth bag that the "roughneck" handed him, he poured a thin layer of sand into his sample tray. Placing the rock cuttings beneath the microscope and carefully adjusting the light mounted upon it, he intently studied the tiny grains of rock. Slowly a grin spread across his face. "Tell the driller to cut ten more feet and then prepare to test. It looks as if we have an oil well on our hands!"

Two thousand miles away—on a dusty, wind-swept mesa in Colorado—another man kneels beside a series of long cylinders of rock. He is looking at cores that have been brought up from

Geologists study the rocky crust in the search for keys to the earth's history.

hundreds of feet beneath the surface. If the dust and 105-degree heat bother this man, you would never know it, for he whistles softly as he pecks away at the core with his hammer and examines first one chip and then another. After making numerous entries in his notebook and placing carefully selected rock samples in a canvas bag, he finally turns toward his jeep. "Box them up, Jim," he tells the core driller. "If these samples look as good in the lab as they do in the field, we've got enough uranium here to provide power for half the country."

Meanwhile, a bearded man hunches over a surveyor's table on a mountainside in Alaska. Alternately looking into his surveyor's instrument and making notations on the sheet of paper on his table, he finally shouts to his partner on the slope below. "O.K., Bob, bring in the rod and get the horses. We should be able to map this entire mountain range from the information that we have gathered this summer."

Three men: one looking through a microscope on a drilling rig off the coast of Texas; one examining a rock core atop a mesa in Colorado; another a map in Alaska. What could they possibly have in common? Geology. Each of these men—for a different reason—was studying the earth.

THE ROAD TO UNDERSTANDING

Not too many years ago the average person had only a vague idea as to the meaning of the term "geology." People living in Texas, Oklahoma, and other oil-producing areas knew that geology had "something to do" with oil. An Arizonan might have suspected that geologists prospected for deposits of copper, Coloradans associated the geologist with the search for uranium, while a resident of Minnesota would have said that a geologist is a man who looks for iron ore. Although geologists do all of these things, in our rapidly expanding and ever-widening world of modern science most people know that geology is the study of the earth. Indeed, the word literally defines itself, for it is derived from the Greek words *geo* (earth) and *logos* (study).

How, you may ask, does the earth scientist study such a complex ball of matter as Earth? What are his problems and how does he attack them? The earth is not only the main object of the geologist's investigations, it is also his laboratory. He examines rock samples for traces of valuable ores, minerals, and fuels that they might contain. He is equally interested in mountains and plains, glaciers and deserts, and the water above and within the ground. The *geoscientist* also studies the many different natural processes that have shaped the face of our earth: the geologic work of ice, wind, and running water. He tries to explain—and, if possible, anticipate—disastrous geologic events such as earthquakes, volcanic eruptions, and landslides. The geoscientist is also concerned about our environment, for problems of pollution, waste disposal, soil erosion, and other environmental concerns are directly related to Earth's air, land, water, and life. As a result, geological studies are relevant to both the cure and prevention of many of our more serious environmental ills.

But the earth scientist is not only interested in Earth as he sees it today—he wants to know where it came from and how

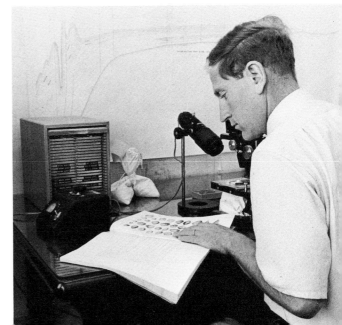

This geological "detective" is using tiny microscopic fossils to determine the age of the rocks that contain them. These fossils may serve as clues to help locate valuable oil-producing rock formations.

it came to be as it is. The solutions to many geological puzzles are locked up in the earth's rocks. To help unravel the mysteries of Earth's exceedingly long history, the geologist studies fossils and the conditions under which life existed in past ages. He uses the prehistoric remains of plants and animals to follow the parade of life from the earliest known bacteria-like organisms of some three billion years ago to the ancestors of modern man. He traces the development of the earth from its origin out of a cloud of dust and gases to the frigid Ice Age which, geologically speaking, ended only yesterday. Neither time nor space discourage the earth scientist. So broad is the area of his interest that it ranges from speculation on the nature of Earth's core hundreds of miles beneath his feet, to research on moon samples collected more than 240,000 miles above him. He delves backward into time to read the dim pages of the geologic past and he reaches forward to theorize on the ultimate fate of our environment. Geology is truly the study of the earth—its past, present, and future.

Though depending largely on the general principles of geology, the earth scientist studies the earth within the framework of many other sciences. From astronomy have come speculations as to the origin of Earth and the other planets in our solar system. And, because minerals and rocks are composed of chemical elements or compounds, chemistry provides knowledge of the composition of the earth. The fundamental principles of physics and mathematics are indispensable, for they help explain the mechanics of earthquakes and solve the mysteries of mountain-building. The biological sciences are equally important. Without knowledge of the plants and animals that are living today, we could not hope to understand the now-vanished forms of the geologic past. Oceanography and meteorology have also made many significant contributions to our comprehension of the earth. So many, in fact, that the study of the oceans and the atmosphere are—along with geology—generally classified as "earth

Apollo 12 Astronaut Alan L. Bean is seen driving a core sample tube into the lunar surface. Samples of lunar rocks may yield clues that will help explain the nature of Earth's original surface.

sciences." Geology, then, is actually a synthesis of sciences—an intriguing body of knowledge that has led to a better understanding of the rather complicated planet that is our home.

GEOLOGISTS AND THEIR WORK

Scientists of today are persistently bombarded with a barrage of new discoveries—a seemingly never-ending series of reports that continually broaden the scope of their research. The result of this unprecedented expansion of knowledge has forced scientists to become increasingly specialized, for it appears that no one scientist can now completely cover any major area of science. Consider, then, the plight of the geologist. His subject is literally world-wide in scope and covers virtually every facet of the earth —not only as we see it today, but Earth as it was in the past and how it might be in the future.

The scope of geological research is so broad that geology has been divided into two general fields: *physical geology* and *historical geology*. Physical geology deals with the structure and composition of the earth and with the physical processes that affect it. However, as earth scientists have learned more about the physical aspects of the earth, additional—but more specialized —fields of geology have arisen. For example, *mineralogists* study the earth's minerals, while rocks are described and classified by *petrographers*. *Vulcanologists* investigate the activities of volcanoes, and *seismologists* try to pinpoint the location of earthquakes and tell us when the next "big one" may hit. The *glaciologist* does research on glaciers and he may literally work from the North to the South Pole. The *structural geologist* puzzles over the cause-and-effect relationships of mountain-building. And as *geochemists* and *geophysicists* analyze the earth in the light of data derived from chemistry and physics, the *geomorphologist* tries to explain the nature, origin, and development of our landscapes.

As a result of the "Space Age," *astrogeology*—a new but growing and promising field of geology—has come into being. Some astrogeologists are involved in mapping the surface of the moon and in other phases of space exploration. In addition, these "space geologists" assist in the training of the Apollo astronauts who are engaged in exploring and sampling the moon.

Recently the *environmental geologist* has appeared. Destined to play a vital role in the future of geology and man, this geological scientist is especially concerned about the conservation of resources and the abuse of our environment. In other words,

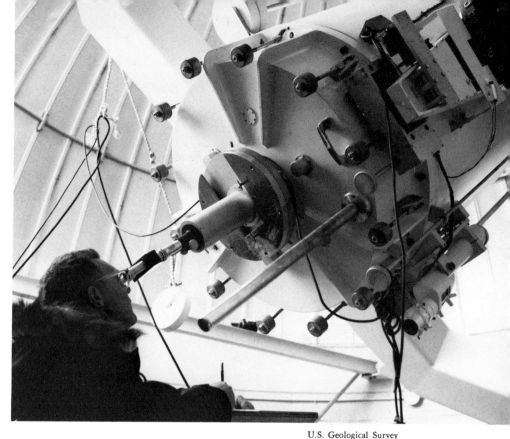

Using the 30-inch reflecting telescope near Flagstaff, Arizona, this astro-geologist is gathering data to compile a map of the moon.

the environmental geoscientist hopes to use geology to answer this vital question: How can man be saved from himself?

The historical geologist, on the other hand, is concerned primarily with the history of the earth—its origin, the many changes that it has undergone, and the history of life as recorded in its rocky crust. This can be fascinating work, for in his role as earth historian the geologist turns detective. Like the astronomer who scans the heavens searching for clues to solve riddles thousands of light-years away, the geologist probes the earth, digging into its crust for evidence that will help unravel the timeless mysteries of the geologic past. In so doing, he plots the position of ancient seas and looks for remnants of lost continents. He traces the slow march of life from the earliest known simple plants, some three

Paleontologists in search of fossils excavate an area in Colorado.

billion years old, through the "Age of Dinosaurs" to ancestral man—a relative newcomer on the geologic scene.

Historical geology, like physical geology, also has its specialized fields of study. The cosmogonist joins the astronomer to make scientific speculations on the birth of the universe and the origin of our earth. By means of fossils buried in the rocks the *paleontologist* traces the history of life on earth and theorizes on the appearance and life habits of long extinct plants and animals. The *stratigrapher*—a specialist in extracting long-buried secrets from the rocks—tries to place the rocks and their prehistoric record in their proper place in geologic time.

Despite the variety of geologic specialties described above, these are but a few of the more specialized fields of investigation undertaken by the earth scientist. They serve to show, however, that geology involves the application of all sciences and scientific methods in the study of the earth and its resources.

Chapter 6

MINERALS, ROCKS, AND THE EARTH'S CRUST

The "ground" beneath us—what could possibly be more familiar? We build our homes on it, much of our food grows in it, and the minerals that build our bodies have been extracted from it. Yet despite our dependence on them, most of us know very little about the rocks and minerals that we call the "ground."

The ground—or more properly the upper part of Earth's solid surface—varies greatly from one place to the next. Many factors produce these differences, but geology and geography are especially important. In the desert the ground is typically covered with loose sand; on the top of Pikes Peak it consists largely of granite; while in the Antarctic it is likely to be composed of glacial ice. What accounts for such striking differences? The material that forms the earth's surface in any particular area is closely related to the rocks that are exposed there. The rocks, in turn, are directly affected by the geologic processes at work in that area.

This suggests, then, that rocks can differ from one place to the next and that they may vary considerably in composition. And they do. It would also seem that different geological processes operate in different parts of the world. This, too, is true. These processes, and the way the local rocks react to them, are responsible for the surface of the desert, the mountaintop, the North Pole—and your own backyard.

Rock and mineral collecting is an increasingly popular hobby with young and old alike.

MINERALS—THE RAW MATERIALS OF ROCK

The word "mineral" means different things to different people. Your family physician may want you to have certain minerals along with your daily vitamin capsule. He might also advise some of his patients to visit areas such as Hot Springs, Arkansas, to bathe in the "mineral" water bubbling from nature's "hot water heater." The prospector panning for gold and the miner working a vein of copper think of mineral in yet another way. To them, minerals are valuable ores from which metal can be extracted.

The earth scientist would agree that certain minerals are vital to good health and that Hot Springs' famous baths might relieve some ailments. And, like the prospector and miner, he would certainly view gold and copper ore as minerals. But to the geologist, minerals are much more basic—he knows them as the stuff from which rocks are made.

Interest in minerals is not confined to geologists. Mineral collecting, or "rockhounding" is quite popular with hobbyists of all ages and people are joining rock and mineral clubs in many parts of the world. As a result, hundreds of books have been written about the various types of minerals, the ways in which they may be identified, and where and how they can be collected. A number of these books are listed on page 202, and hopefully the reader will be inspired to probe more deeply into this popular and fascinating topic.

In this introduction to the earth we are taking a rather broad view of the world of geology. Consequently, we cannot describe in detail the many different types of minerals or discuss their distinctive physical properties. On the other hand, the solid earth *is* composed of rocks and these rocks *are* composed of minerals. Clearly, they have a place in a book about the earth. But rather than merely catalog the names and properties of minerals, let us find out *why* there are so many different kinds of minerals. Equally important, what determines the physical and chemical properties that characterize the various mineral species?

Minerals, like all matter, are made up of minute particles called *atoms*. Each of these indivisible specks of matter has its own unique chemical composition and physical properties. We might compare the various kinds of atoms to the different species, or kinds, of animals. Every animal species has certain distinguishing features that make it possible to tell, for example, the difference between a lion and a Siamese kitten. Both of these animals have certain catlike features in common—but they are quite clearly two different "breeds of cat." By the same token, the different kinds of atoms have distinctive features which relate them to one specific *element*. In other words, each element is composed exclusively of one special type of atom: gold is composed of gold atoms, oxygen of oxygen atoms, and so on down the line.

The chemical elements are quite literally the building blocks of our planet. Earth's liquids, solids, and gases, plus all plant and animal life, consist of definite combinations of ninety natural elements that occur on the earth and in the air. There are, in addition, at least fifteen man-made elements.

Interestingly enough, almost three-fourths—74.3 per cent, to be exact—of the earth's crust consists of only two elements: oxygen and silicon. And, as you will see in the table below, almost 98.6 per cent of the crust (by weight) consists of these two elements plus six more.

AVERAGE CHEMICAL COMPOSITION OF THE EARTH'S CRUST

Element	Symbol	Percentage by Weight	Percentage by Volume
Oxygen	O	46.60	93.8
Silicon	Si	27.72	0.9
Aluminum	Al	8.13	0.5
Iron	Fe	5.00	0.4
Calcium	Ca	3.63	1.0
Sodium	Na	2.83	1.3
Potassium	K	2.59	1.8
Magnesium	Mg	2.09	0.3
All others	—	1.41	—
TOTAL		100.00	100.0

Oxygen is an element that is familiar to most of us, for we know that we must breathe this gas in order to live. It is not surprising, then, that many people are astonished to learn that oxygen is *not* the most abundant element in the atmosphere. And, because oxygen is generally thought of as a gas, they are even more surprised to learn that oxygen *is* extremely abundant in

Jennie A. Matthews

Rock-forming minerals such as this crystalline quartz make up an important part of the earth's crust.

the solid earth. More specifically, 93.8 per cent of the earth's crust, by volume, and 46.6 per cent of the crust, by weight, consists of oxygen.

This is possible because the oxygen atom is so much larger than the atoms of the other more common elements. In fact, we can visualize the earth's crust as a skeleton of oxygen atoms with the smaller atoms of other elements neatly tucked in the spaces between them.

How do the remaining eighty-two natural elements fit into the crust? If altogether they only make up 1.41 per cent of the crust by weight, they must be relatively rare. Consider, for example, such apparently "common" elements as lead and copper. Lead constitutes only 0.0015 per cent and copper 0.0045 per cent of the crust. And gold certainly deserves its description as a "rare metal," considering that it makes up an infinitesimal 0.000007 per cent of the crustal rocks!

Although elements commonly combine chemically to produce a *compound*, they may also occur alone. In this respect, the chemical elements are somewhat like the letters of our alphabet. They are occasionally used separately but are more often brought together in various combinations to form words. We can compare a mineral to a word. In our language we unite letters to create a word, and nature combines certain chemical elements to form a particular mineral. One common mineral, for example, always consists of equal proportions of the same two elements: sodium and chlorine. Chemists call this compound sodium chloride. The mineralogist has named it *halite*. However, when you refer to this mineral, it is probably to say, "Please pass the salt."

Just as the letters "a" and "I" are frequently used alone, certain minerals contain but a single element. Diamond (which consists of carbon), sulfur, and gold are some minerals which commonly occur in a *native* or *elemental* state. Does this mean that all elements and compounds are minerals? No indeed. The "membership requirements" in Nature's "Mineral Club" are quite restrictive. To begin with, the substance must occur naturally—it cannot be synthetically produced or man-made. It must also be inorganic; that is, it cannot be, or have been, part of any living thing. A mineral must also have a definite chemical composition and possess certain distinctive physical characteristics.

Despite these rather rigorous requirements, more than 2000 "members" have joined the "club," for this many minerals have been named and described. Fortunately for professional and amateur "rockhounds," each mineral has its own distinctive physical characteristics. But, as in plant and animal species, there

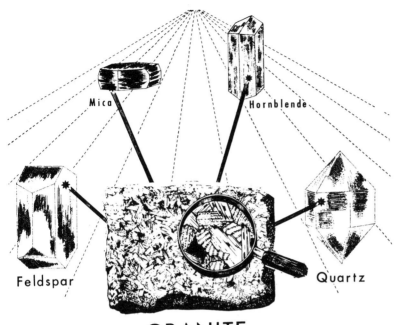

Mica

Hornblende

Feldspar

Quartz

GRANITE

Bureau of Economic Geology, The University of Texas

The most common igneous rock, granite, consists mostly of quartz and feldspar. However, other minerals such as mica and hornblende are commonly present.

may be minor variations from one specimen to the next.

How can we tell one mineral from another? We use our natural senses to identify the objects around us and to distinguish between them. Sight tells us that a mouse and an elephant are not alike. A rose has one scent, while a gardenia has another. Sugar has a sweet taste; salt does not. Some materials have a rough texture and others are smooth to the touch.

Our senses can also be used to determine the physical and chemical properties that distinguish one mineral from another. The "trademark" of halite (rock salt) is its salty taste. Diamond, on the other hand, is noted for its brilliant luster and extreme hardness. Such unique characteristics are the exception rather than the rule, however, for most minerals must be identified by a combination of several properties.

A mineral's more distinctive features—its crystal form, hardness, or specific gravity, for example—are expressed externally. That is, we can see the shape of the crystal, scratch the mineral to determine its hardness, or weigh it to determine its specific gravity. Yet as obvious as these external features may be, they are produced by the internal structure of the mineral. The kind of atoms present, their relative proportions, and the way in which they are arranged are all involved.

The chemical composition of a mineral can also be traced back to its atoms. Chemically, the mineral is what its atoms are composed of. Oxygen and silicon are by far the most abundant crustal elements; thus they are found in large numbers of minerals. Known as the *silicates*, about thirteen of these oxygen and silicon-bearing rocks make up most of the earth's crust. Because of their value as builders of rocks, the silicates are also called the *rock-forming minerals*.

ROCKS FORM THE LAND

Considering how common rocks are it is astonishing how little we appreciate their importance in our daily lives. Worse yet, we are not always too complimentary in referring to them. We describe certain individuals as having a "heart of stone," a "stony countenance," being as "hard as a rock"—even as having "rocks in their heads!"

Perhaps rocks are *too* common, for like such vital essentials as air and water, they are usually taken for granted. Not by the geologist, however. Rocks are his "stock-in-trade," for geology is based on the study of rocks. These rocks and stones are important in everyone's life. Ore-bearing rocks contain the metals so vital to industry; other rocks are used to make cement, tile, bricks, and glass; "rock oil," or petroleum, provides fuel for heat

Ward's Natural Science Establishment

Galena, an important ore of lead, is a typical metallic mineral.

and power; more important, rocks break down to form soils that produce our food—the list is endless. The different *kinds* of rocks also seem to be endless, for they occur in such amazing variety and numbers. Yet despite their many differences, all of Earth's rocks have one thing in common: minerals.

You will recall that we have compared Earth's chemical elements to the letters of the alphabet and its minerals to "words" formed from them. Using this same analogy, we can compare rocks to sentences. We assemble words to form sentences and nature combines minerals to form rocks. The sentence you are now reading contains nine words. This sentence consists of six words. These two sentences differ in the number and kinds of words in them and rocks differ in the kinds and amounts of minerals that they contain. Some, such as rock salt, contain only one mineral. Other rocks, such as granite, are made up of several minerals. In other words, the kinds, sizes, and quantities of minerals and the way that the mineral constituents are held together

The landscape at Craters of the Moon National Monument in Idaho is composed of extrusive or volcanic igneous rocks.

will determine the appearance and physical properties of a rock.

The next time you go for a walk pick up several rocks and examine them carefully. You will probably notice that some rocks contain many specks of color of different shapes and sizes. These may be the minerals in the rock, for many minerals do not lose their identity when they combine to form rocks.

Mineral composition is very important in the study of rocks, but it does not form the fundamental basis for rock classification. Instead, rocks are placed in one of three rock families, according to how they were formed. Each of these rock groups— igneous, sedimentary, and metamorphic—makes its own special contribution to the solid matter of Earth's crust.

The igneous rocks get their name from the Latin word *ignis*, meaning "fire." These "fire-formed" rocks are the ancestors of all other rocks, for they appear to have been the first rocks to form on Earth. They have been produced by the cooling and hardening of molten rock material called *magma*. A mixture of melted minerals, magma forms deep within the earth where it accumulates in pockets or magma reservoirs.

Some of the magma rises to the surface through volcanoes to form *lava*. Lava, and other igneous rocks that cool and solidify on the earth's surface, are called *extrusive* or volcanic rocks. We will have more to say about these in a later chapter.

Other igneous rocks have formed from magma injected into rocks buried deep within the earth. These *intrusive*, or *plutonic*, igneous rocks are typically seen in areas that have undergone much erosion. Here, the intrusive masses have been raised near the surface by movements within the earth. As time passed, they were eventually exposed as the overlying rocks were gradually weathered and worn away. This is why you can see plutonic rocks in such contrasting places as the deep inner gorge of the Grand Canyon or the lofty summit of Pikes Peak.

Granite, the most common igneous rock, is generally considered to be plutonic in origin. Yet some geologists are not so sure. They argue that certain masses of granitic rock are much too large to have been injected into the surrounding rock. Such granite bodies—the Coast Ranges of British Columbia, for example—are so massive that they might have formed in place by the process of *granitization*. Other geologists doubt that this little-understood process even exists. Thus, the true origin of this commonest of all "igneous" rock remains one of Earth's more puzzling unsolved mysteries.

Igneous rocks become increasingly abundant in the deeper parts of the earth, for about 95 per cent of the volume of the outermost ten miles of the crust consists of rocks of igneous origin. They are much less common, however, on the surface of the earth.

Sedimentary rocks are composed of loose rock fragments

Devils Tower in Wyoming is a good example of intrusive or plutonic rocks that cooled in the crust and were later exposed by erosion.

called *sediments*. These sediments consist of weathered rock and mineral grains such as mud, sand, and gravel. With the passage of time, the sediments have hardened into layers, or *strata*, of sedimentary rock. Because of the bedded, or layered, nature of these rocks, they are also known as stratified rocks.

Sediments formed from the breakdown and decay of previously existing rocks have usually been moved from their place of origin. Wind, running water, and glaciers transport rock particles from one area and deposit them elsewhere. The more common rocks around us—sandstone, clay, and some limestones—are typical sedimentary rocks. Other sedimentary rocks consist of the remains or products of ancient plants and animals. Coal and fossil-bearing limestones have formed in this way. Sedimentary rocks may also be created as a result of chemical reactions. Rock salt, gypsum, and certain other chemically produced sedimentary rocks have been precipitated from solution in sea water.

Unlike igneous rocks, which may originate either within the crust or on Earth's surface, sedimentary rocks form on or very near the surface of the earth. As a result, only some 5 per cent of the outer ten miles of the crust consists of sedimentary rocks. By contrast, sedimentary rocks make up almost 75 per cent of the earth's surface rocks. These rocks are an important source of mineral resources such as salt, water, sulfur, and petroleum. They also break down to form some of our more fertile soils. The historical geologist is especially interested in sedimentary rocks, for they commonly contain fossils. These traces of prehistoric organisms and other sedimentary features are clues that help reveal much of the history of the earth.

The third great rock family consists of the metamorphic rocks. They get their name from two Greek words which literally mean "change in form." This is a very good name, for they consist of earlier-formed igneous or sedimentary rocks that have been changed into new and quite different rocks. The process of

Geology Department, Lamar University

Composed of rock fragments called sediment, sedimentary rocks are characterized by their layering or stratification. Here, the layers have been tilted upward as a result of movements in the crust.

Metamorphic rocks have been greatly altered by intense heat and pressure. The minerals in this piece of gneiss have been contorted due to rock flowage.

metamorphism may alter sedimentary limestone into the metamorphic rock called marble, or change sandstone into much harder quartzite.

Metamorphism occurs below the surface of the earth where rocks may be affected by intense pressure and heat. These changes can be produced when rocks are squeezed, bent, or broken during crustal disturbances such as mountain-building. Deeply buried rocks can also be invaded by mineral-bearing liquids and gases from nearby concentrations of magma. As these fluids seep into the surrounding rock, original minerals may be dissolved and new ones will form in their place. Some of these minerals, such as gold and silver, may enrich rocks that were originally of little economic value.

These "made-over" rocks are especially common in areas

where the rocks have been baked by igneous intrusions or deformed by severe crustal movements. And, because of the conditions under which they formed, the metamorphic rocks provide evidence of some of the more violent chapters in earth history.

EARTH'S ROCKY "SKIN"

Our planet's rocky "skin" forms a very thin veneer on the earth's surface. In a way it is somewhat like the rind of an orange which represents but a small fraction of the orange's diameter. The earth's "rind" represents, at the very most, less than forty miles of the almost 4,000 miles to the center of the earth. So, on a comparative basis, Earth's "skin" is much thinner than the covering of an orange.

The rocks in the earth's crust occur in different ways. Some rock is in the form of loose surface material such as sand, gravel, or soil. This is the *mantle rock*. The *bedrock*—a continuous mass of solid rock that has not yet been disturbed by surface agents of weathering and erosion—lies beneath the mantle rock.

Although they appear to differ greatly, the bedrock and mantle rock are closely related. One may be considered the product of the other, for mantle rock consists of rock debris derived from the weathering and erosion of the solid bedrock. On the other hand, loose fragments of the mantle rock may eventually become packed and cemented together to become bedrock.

In the next chapter we will take a closer look at the composition and arrangement of Earth's crustal rocks. We will also attempt to peel back the crust to see what lies bneath our planet's rocky skin.

Chapter 7

INSIDE STORY—
CRUST, MANTLE, AND CORE

On any given day millions of people walk or ride over Earth's solid surface. Countless others sail on its waters, while airplanes cruise through the atmosphere above them all. Man has invaded all parts of our earthly environment and has—at long last—finally come to appreciate the role of earth materials in our lives.

As he has searched for places to live and materials to use, man has ranged far and wide over the face of the earth. The need for space and his natural curiosity have driven him from the equator to the Arctic and from the ocean floor to the tops of mountains. We have even left our home planet and traveled almost a quarter of a million miles to explore the surface of the moon.

But despite our familiarity with the face of the earth and our curiosity about the moon, puzzling mysteries still remain locked within this rocky globe. Indeed, in many ways we know considerably more about the secrets of interstellar space than we do about the mysterious realm of "inner space" that lies beneath our feet.

Spacecraft have carried man to the moon and deep-sea submersibles have permitted him to prowl the ocean depths. If astronauts can explore space and aquanauts roam the sea floor, will "lithonauts" someday probe the inner reaches of the earth?

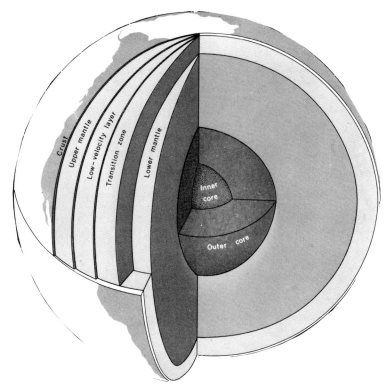

U.S. Geological Survey

This cross-section of our planet shows the postulated arrangement of the earth's interior.

Surely the technology that has rocketed spacemen 240,000 miles to the moon can send a man less than 4000 miles to the center of the earth. Engineers do not easily accept defeat and scientists are not quick to say "No" to even the most difficult question. Even so, both scientist and engineers reluctantly admit that such a trip is highly unlikely in the foreseeable future.

Consider the problems. Imagine the highly specialized type of device that would be needed to bore through thousands of miles of solid rock. This stony barrier not only becomes hotter with depth, the deeper rocks are subjected to increasingly tremendous pressure. The pressure at the center of the earth is about 3 ½ million times greater than the atmospheric pressure at Earth's surface. The temperature? The heat within the earth gradually rises with depth until it may reach 4000 to 5000 degrees Fahrenheit—almost half as hot as the surface of the sun!

The deepest hole ever drilled—an unsuccessful oil test in Texas —penetrated the earth for about five miles. The Mohole, an ill-fated attempt to drill through Earth's outer crust, did not get this deep. Both of these ventures encountered serious drilling problems at great depth. Then, too, consider the hostile environment that a lithonaut would encounter. It would take a most remarkable inner-space vehicle to protect him from the crush of subterranean pressures and the searing heat of the surrounding rocks.

X-RAYING EARTH'S ANATOMY

How, then, can scientists explore inner space? Oddly enough, most of what we know about Earth's interior has been learned from the study of earthquakes. This may surprise you, for we normally think of earthquakes in terms of demolished buildings, loss of life, and similar destructions. But even an earthquake has its "good" side, for earthquake, or *seismic*, waves have provided valuable clues as to the nature of Earth's interior.

Seismology—the study of earthquakes—is a fascinating branch of geology and we will learn more about earthquakes in the next chapter. Meanwhile, it will be helpful to know something about the nature of seismic waves and how they carry their "messages" to the geologist.

Like X-rays, seismic waves penetrate the solid materials of the earth. And just as X-rays tell us something about that part of our anatomy that we cannot see with our naked eye, seismic waves provide us with an "X-ray picture" of Earth's internal structure.

It has long been known that earthquake waves are transmitted through the earth. It is also known that these waves travel at

Environmental Science Services Administration

Seismographs such as this one detect earthquake waves that reveal much about the earth's interior.

different speeds through rocks of different physical and chemical composition. Of the two types of waves transmitted through the earth, the fastest are the *compression*, or *push*, waves. They move faster in deeper parts of the earth and travel at velocities (speeds) of from 3.4 to 8.6 miles per second. Because they are the first waves to be recorded by the *seismograph* (a sensitive instrument designed to record earthquake vibrations), they are also called P or primary waves. The *transverse*, or *shear*, waves are a bit slower, passing through the earth at velocities which range from 2.2 to 4.5 miles per second. They are also called S, or secondary, waves because they are the second set of waves to be detected by the seismograph.

Seismic waves travel faster through very dense rock than through lighter rocks. Consequently, the speed of the earthquake wave may provide information about the nature of the rock through which it passes. Seismologists also know that earthquake waves are deflected, or change direction at certain depths within the earth. The depths at which the waves are deflected indicate changes in the rock at the depth where the waves change their path. Studies of the P and S waves have permitted earth scientists to divide the earth's interior into three rather clearly defined zones—the crust, the mantle, and the core.

WHEN A CRUST IS NOT A CRUST

Early geologists thought that the inside of our globe was filled with hot, molten rock. They also assumed that the earth's solid surface consisted of a rocky crust that formed as the upper part of the melted rock slowly cooled. And why not? It was a well-known fact that this solid crust would occasionally crack open, permitting molten rock to spill out over the land. Thus, volcanoes and their lavas seemed to prove this conception of the earth's interior. We now know that this early idea was wrong. Even so, geologists still use the term "crust" to refer to the outer rigid part of the lithosphere.

Thanks to seismologists, we now have a good idea as to the true nature of the crust. Compared to the rest of our planet the crustal shell is rather thin. It is as little as three miles thick under parts of the ocean basins to as much as thirty miles thick beneath the higher mountains. These rocks are not arranged in one flat, homogeneous layer. There are, instead, distinct differences in density, thickness, and composition. And, although of great importance to man, the crustal rocks make up only about 1 per cent of Earth's volume, so they are minor constitutents in the over-all makeup of our planet.

There is considerable difference between the *oceanic* crust that forms the ocean floors and the *continental* crust that makes up the landmasses. The crust beneath the sea is rather uniform in composition. It consists mostly of very dense basaltic rocks similar to those commonly erupted from volcanoes. By contrast, the more complex continental crust appears to be made up of two rather distinct layers: an upper layer of light-colored rocks

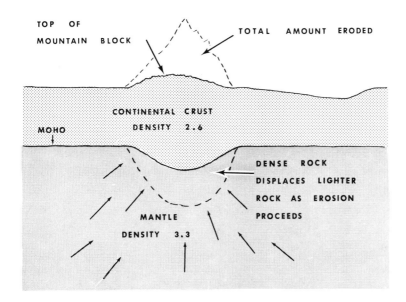

Because the rocks are less dense, the continental crust seems to "float" on the heavier rocks of the underlying mantle.

similar to granite and a lower zone of dark, somewhat denser basaltic rock.

Geologists were originally puzzled by the difference in thickness of the oceanic and continental crust. It is now known, however, that the lighter granitic crustal rocks literally float on the heavier basaltic rocks beneath them. Some parts of the "floating" crust have sunk more deeply into the earth than others. This is especially true under great mountain ranges where the thickened crust reaches deeply down into the more plastic rocks that support them. Continental areas of low elevation also "float." But these thinner segments of the continental crust do not send down "roots" like those that develop under mountains. Density, or the weight of the rocks, also has a hand in determining how thick the crust shall be. The lighter weight of the granitic rocks of the continental crust permits them to "float" higher than the more dense underlying rocks of the oceanic crust.

THE MOHO AND THE MANTLE

The year was 1909, and Professor Andrija Mohorovičić was studying seismograph records of an earthquake that had rocked the Zagreb, Yugoslavia, area on October 8. As his work progressed, Mohorovičić made a startling discovery—at certain depths within the earth, seismic waves abruptly change direction and increase in speed. Further study of records from widely scattered seismograph stations eventually led Mohorovičić to conclude that the change in seismic wave behavior is due to a corresponding change in the rocks through which the waves have passed. He found that seismic waves travel more slowly near the surface because of the rigidity of the crustal rocks. But at the base of the crust the rocks are less rigid, thus permitting the waves to speed up and change their paths.

This important discovery actually proved the presence of the crust and provided seismologists with a means of determining its thickness. The transitional zone at the base of the crust has been named the Mohorovičić Discontinuity or Moho, in honor of the man who first detected it.

What causes such an abrupt change in the seismic waves as they cross the boundary of the Moho? The waves are entering the mantle, an 1800-mile-thick layer of very dense, solid rock. As the waves continue through the mantle some of them are reflected back to the surface. This, plus other changes in the behavior of the waves, suggests that the mantle is layered.

Because it is impossible to sample the deeply buried rocks of the mantle, we can only speculate about their composition. However, they appear to be composed of igneous rocks that are rich in iron and magnesium. This speculation has been strengthened by studies of rock samples found in certain volcanic rocks collected in Hawaii and Antarctica. These eruptive materials contain minerals that may be fragments of the mantle which have been carried to the surface by magma.

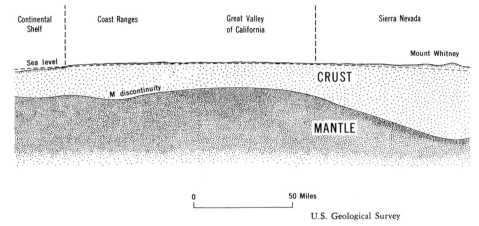

Cross-section of the continental crust under California, showing the location of the Mohorovičić Discontinuity.

THE "HEART" OF THE EARTH

At a depth of about 1800 miles, seismic waves relay yet another message to the surface. Their actions at this point reveal a drastic change as they enter the core of our planet. About 4350 miles in diameter, the core is completely enclosed by the mantle.

The pattern established by the P and S waves suggests that the core consists of two parts. The *outer core,* which is about 1300 miles thick, begins at the base of the mantle and reaches to a depth of about 3160 miles. This part of the core appears to consist of liquid rock material. Beneath this, with a diameter of some 1700 miles, lies the solid *inner core.*

Like most of what we know about inner space, seismic messages have provided an explanation of the twofold division of the heart of our planet. When P waves pass through the outer core they slow down quite suddenly and behave as if they are traveling through a liquid. But upon reaching the inner core, the P waves abruptly resume their speed and act as if they are again passing through a solid. Even more significant is the reaction of the S waves, for this type of seismic wave cannot pass

Personnel at Hawaii Volcano Observatory extract a core of lava from beneath crust of hardened lava "lake." Samples of this type may contain some indication of the nature of deeper crustal rocks from which the lava originates.

through a liquid. The fact that they cannot pass through the center of the earth is thought to be further proof of the liquid nature of the core's outer shell.

Although seismic waves have provided clues as to the arrangement of the core, many questions still surround its composition. It is believed, however, to consist of very dense rocks composed of about 80 per cent iron with varying amounts of nickel, silicon, and cobalt. This, incidentally, is similar to the composition of certain meteorite fragments, which may represent the remains of disintegrated Earthlike planets.

Such is the "X-ray picture" of our planet's anatomy. This view of Earth's interior has enabled the geologist to develop a mental model of the earth's internal structure. Although this standard model is generally accepted today, many mysteries are still tightly sealed in the rocks of the deep interior. Indeed, questions about the earth still far exceed the available answers.

Chapter 8

SHIVERS AND SPASMS
WITHIN THE EARTH

April 18, 1906, is a date that will long live in the history of California. It was shortly after 5:00 A.M., on this fateful Wednesday that the residents of San Francisco were rolled out of their beds quite unexpectedly. As they opened their eyes they were greeted by the crash of collapsing buildings, violent shaking of the ground, and the clanging of church bells as steeples swayed with the trembling earth. Worse yet, fires were soon started as chimneys toppled and stoves were upset. Firehouses were demolished and water mains ruptured, allowing the flames to roar unchecked for three days. When the dust had settled and the last wisps of smoke had finally drifted away, the still-dazed San Franciscans surveyed their surroundings in disbelief. Almost five hundred city blocks had been laid waste. Some quarter of a million people were left without homes, and thirty schools, eighty churches, the City Hall, and most of the city's public buildings were in ruins. The earthquake and fires were responsible for more than 600 deaths and property damage was in the neighborhood of $400 million.

W H Y ?

We now know that the historic San Francisco earthquake is but one of countless temblors that have rocked our planet for

A view of the Knob Hill area of San Francisco as it appeared following the 1906 earthquake and fire.

billions of years. But the ancients did not know this. They explained these awesome, earth-shattering catastrophes in the light of legend and superstition. The lamas of Mongolia thought that our earth was supported by a frog. Each time the frog moved or croaked the earth would vibrate, thus causing an earthquake. But the early Greeks and Romans had their own ideas. They visualized the earth as a hollow ball filled with gas. Earthquakes were produced by pressures generated when the trapped gas escaped to the surface. The ancient Hindus had a more complicated explanation. The earth, they said, rested on the backs of elephants. The elephants stood on the shell of a giant turtle which rested, in turn, on a coiled cobra. Movement of these mythical animals would upset Earth's balance, thereby causing an earthquake.

The damage at San Francisco was not caused, of course, by jostling animals or trapped gas bursting though Earth's crust.

Seismologists believe that earthquakes are triggered by *faults*—a type of earth fracture that occurs when subsurface rocks are suddenly broken and displaced.

We have seen that the more deeply buried rocks are constantly subjected to great stress and strain. These pressures build up as time passes and the rocks are gradually deformed and bent. But even the strongest rock must eventually reach its breaking point and it is then that faulting occurs. This sudden fracture—and the abrupt displacement of the rocks along the fracture, or *fault plane*—generates wavelike motions in the rocks. These are called seismic waves, from the Greek word *seismos* which means "earthquake."

The tremors that leveled much of San Francisco lasted but about sixty seconds. Yet it probably took the subsurface rocks thousands—even millions—of years to reach their breaking point. The damage was caused by vibrations generated when the rocks snapped back into their original unstrained position.

This explanation of the fracture and "snapping back" of the rocks is known as the *elastic rebound theory*. Interestingly enough, evidence gathered from the 1906 San Francisco earthquake was used to formulate this now generally accepted explanation of how seismic waves are generated. Here is further evidence that some benefit may be derived from even the most destructive earth phenomena.

Most quakes are associated with active faults where two parts of the earth's crust have slipped with respect to each other. Structures of this type are most likely to occur in areas where there has been some recent crustal disturbance such as mountain-building or volcanic activity. One such fracture, the San Andreas Fault, slices through the earth's crust for hundreds of miles along the western border of California. The 1906 San Francisco disaster and a number of California's other destructive temblors have been caused by movements along the San Andreas Fault.

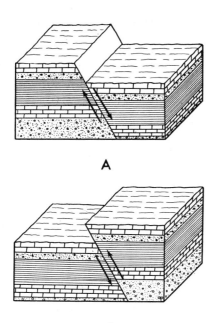

A

B

Faulting is believed to be the basic cause of most earthquakes. In a normal fault (A) the movement is down the dip, or slope, of the fault plane. In a reverse fault (B) the movement is up the dip of the fault plane.

There are many "splinter faults" or offshoots of the San Andreas Fault. One of these was responsible for the destructive earthquake which jolted the San Fernando, California, area early on the morning of February 9, 1971. This temblor took sixty-four lives and did more than one billion dollars in property damage—in a matter of sixty seconds! Luckily, the initial shock struck at 6:01 A.M. Consequently, the resulting loss of life and injuries was much less than if the quake had occurred one or two hours later. At that time of day freeways would have been clogged with traffic, and schools and offices would have been filled.

Earthquakes do not occur indiscriminantly throughout the world. Instead, they are restricted to rather clearly defined

The February, 1971, earthquake that struck the San Fernando Valley of California did great damage to Olive View Hospital which is shown here.

seismic belts or zones. The largest of these, the circum-Pacific Belt is a storm center of seismic shocks, for it spawns 80 per cent of the world's earthquakes. A zone of young mountain ranges and volcanic cones, this zone reaches from Chile along the west-

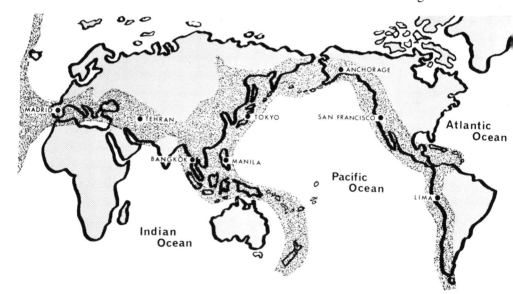

Major earthquake "belts" of the world.

View of downtown Anchorage, Alaska, after the Good Friday Earthquake of 1964.

ern borders of South and North America, northward to the
Aleutians and Alaska. It also includes Japan, the Philippines,
New Zealand, Indonesia, and certain Pacific islands.

The Mediterranean and trans-Asiatic belt extends from the
Atlantic Ocean, through the Mediterranean area to the southern
part of Eurasia. Approximately 15 per cent of all earthquakes
occur in this belt. The remaining 5 per cent of earthquakes are
scattered throughout other parts of the world.

Do you live in "earthquake country?" If your home is in
California the answer is clearly "Yes!" If you live in the states
of Alaska, Nevada, Utah, or Montana, the reply is "Maybe."
But even though you don't live in or near an active seismic area
you might still experience an earthquake. Such unlikely places
as South Carolina, Illinois, Missouri, Tennessee, New York, and
the New England area have been jolted by earthquakes of varying intensities.

EARTHQUAKE DAMAGE

August 17, 1959, is known as "the night the mountain moved"
to the residents of West Yellowstone, Montana. It was shortly
after midnight on this date that an earthquake jarred loose a
chunk of mountain more than 1300 feet wide and 2000 feet long.
Rushing down a steep canyon wall at a speed of about 100 miles
per hour, this great landslide contained between 30 and 50 million cubic yards of rock. It ground to a halt on the valley floor
and formed a natural dam across the Madison River. At least
twenty-eight lives were lost in his tragedy and nineteen bodies
still lie beneath some 200 feet of rock that fills the canyon floor.

Landslides such as this are but one of the ways that earthquakes
damage the land. Earth spasms commonly cause gaping cracks
to open up, especially where surface materials are loose and
unconsolidated. *Fault scarps*—clifflike features which are surface

U. S. Geological Survey

Some earth movements—like the disastrous Madison River Canyon landslide in Montana—move with incredible speed and do great damage. The lake in the foreground formed when the slide debris dammed the river.

evidence of the faulting that caused the quake—may also be developed.

Earth's waters, like the land, are commonly disturbed by seismic vibrations. Streams tumble over fault scarps to form waterfalls and stream beds may be offset and channels changed as a result of lateral movement of the surface. Seismic vibrations can also produce water movement called a *seiche* (saysh). This may cause the water in a lake or pond to slosh back and forth as if in a pan. The large earthquake that struck Alaska in 1964 agitated water in swimming pools in such distant places as Texas and Louisiana, and generated waves six feet high in the Gulf of Mexico!

Earthquakes that occur beneath the sea—and luckily most of them do—occasionally generate great waves of water called *tsunamis* (soo-nahm-ees). A tsunami associated with the great Lisbon, Portugal, earthquake of 1755 reached an estimated height of fifty feet and smashed inland for more than one-half mile.

Known also as seismic sea waves, these killer-waves may travel at speeds of up to 500 miles per hour and be as much as a hundred feet high. These giant waves appear to be generated by massive vertical displacements on the ocean floor as a result of faulting or volcanic explosions. Such was the case when the East Indies volcano, Krakatoa, literally "blew its top" in 1883. The series of tsunamis generated by the explosion and collapse of this volcano killed approximately 36,500 people. A ship docked in

The great tsunami generated by Alaska's 1964 earthquake tossed trucks, buses, and trains about like toys.

U. S. Geological Survey

the area was washed about one mile inland and left high and dry some thirty feet above sea level.

History has proven that the aftereffects of an earthquake can be as destructive as the quake itself. As in the San Francisco earthquake, fire caused by clogged chimneys and overturned stoves is one of the greatest hazards. In the devastating Japanese earthquake of 1923, post-earthquake fires leveled 71 per cent of the houses in Tokyo and 65 per cent of those in Yokahama. Damaged water supplies not only hamper fire fighting, but drinking water may become contaminated. This, plus food spoilage and other health and sanitation problems, may give rise to epidemics and the spread of disease, thus causing additional loss of life.

Unfortunately, not all the problems created by earthquakes are physical. Serious emotional and psychological disorders have been known to affect certain people who have experienced the nightmarish experience of even a "moderate" temblor. Aftershocks—relatively minor tremors that may follow the main earthquake shock—caused severe cases of "earthquake jitters" among many people involved in the 1971 San Fernando Valley quake. Many children were afraid to leave their parents, and some home owners literally walked away, leaving their shattered homes forever.

SEISMIC WAVES AND WHAT THEY TELL US

As noted in the last chapter, seismic waves have revealed much about the inside of our planet. Such information is largely provided by the P and S waves which pass through the earth's interior. The third type of seismic wave, the L or long waves, are generated from energy produced by the P and S waves. Because they travel relatively slowly—about 2.2 miles per second—these are the last waves to be detected by the seismograph. And, because they pass through the surface rocks, they are also the most destructive.

The seismograph is something of a mechanical watchman that is constantly on the alert for earthquake waves. A typical seismograph consists of a spring-suspended weight or pendulum that is free to swing in the direction of the waves to be recorded. The frame to which the pendulum is attached is firmly anchored in solid bedrock. The pendulum supports a mirror that reflects a thin beam of light on a roll of light-sensitive photographic paper. The paper is attached to a revolving cylinder that is operated by clockwork.

When the crust is at rest the light "writes" on the paper in a rather uniform line. But vibrations in the earth will activate the pendulum, producing a wavy or jagged line on the paper. The resulting record, called a *seismogram*, provides a tracing that will reveal the various types of seismic waves and the times that they were detected by the instrument.

If suitable seismograms can be obtained from properly located seismograph stations, they can be used to track down the site of the disturbance. They can also tell us when the earthquake occurred.

Seismograms can provide clues as to the *hypocenter*, or *focus*, of the earthquake. This is the point *within* the earth from which the shocks originate. Seismic records can also be used to detect the earthquake's *epicenter*—the point on the earth's *surface* which lies directly above the hypocenter. This information can be obtained by making a comparative study of the behavior and arrival times of the different kinds of seismic waves.

Seismic waves spread out from the hypocenter the instant an earthquake strikes. These waves vary greatly in amplitude (size) and velocity. The first waves to be detected are the relatively mild P waves, and the stronger S waves follow closely behind them. Last—but certainly not least—the devastating L waves record their ominous zigzag pattern on the recording drum.

By studying the different arrival times of the various types of

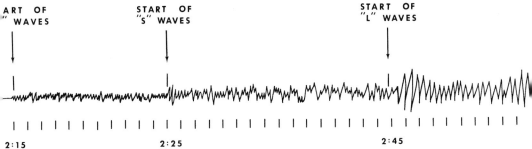

ART OF
"" WAVES

START OF
"s" WAVES

START OF
"L" WAVES

2:15   2:25   2:45

TIME IN MINUTES

Typical seismogram showing arrival times of seismic waves in minutes.

seismic waves, the seismologist can determine the distance to the epicenter. More important, if records from at least three strategically situated seismograph stations are available, it is possible to determine the exact geographic location of the epicenter. To do this, circles are drawn for three seismic observatories, with the station in the exact center of each circle. The point at which the three circles intersect each other will denote the earthquake's epicenter.

Seismic studies indicate that about 85 per cent of all earthquakes are *shallow focus* quakes that are born from ten to thirty miles below the surface. On the other hand, the so-called *deep focus* quakes may originate as much as 435 miles within the earth. Consequently, the seismologist not only wants to know "when" and "where," he also asks: "How deep?" The answer is again supplied by the seismogram, for the depth of focus can be determined by calculating the difference in arrival times of the P, S, and L waves.

HOW EARTHQUAKES ARE MEASURED

Some earthquakes are described as "small," while more destructive seismic events are said to be "large" or "major" earthquakes.

Such descriptions are quite relative, for we have already seen how damaging a so-called "moderate" earthquake can be. What determines the size of an earthquake? Seismologists normally measure earthquakes according to their intensity or magnitude.

Earthquake intensity is measured in terms of the amount of physical damage or geologic change produced by the quake. In short, the intensity of the quake is a measure of the destruction caused in a given area. Estimates of earthquake intensity are usually made by experienced observers and based on the amount of physical change in a specified location. Such estimates are, of course, relative and subjective.

American seismologists generally use the Modified Mercalli Intensity Scale to indicate varying degrees of intensity. This scale uses roman numerals to designate twelve classes of observable effects. An intensity of I is so slight as to be detected only by instruments or under very favorable circumstances. At the other extreme is XII—an earthquake of such intensity that total destruction is produced. Most quakes lie somewhere between these two extremes.

An earthquake's magnitude—the amount of energy released by the quake—is measured by more objective and quantitative means. This measurement rules out the human element, for it is based on instrument recordings of the size or amplitude of the seismic waves. The Richter Scale (which uses a series of Arabic numerals) is used to denote earthquake magnitude. These numbers are related to the actual energy released in the bedrock of the earth.

An earthquake rated at 2.5 on the Richter Scale would hardly be noticed. But a quake of magnitude 7 could be felt over an area of 50,000 square miles and would be capable of doing much damage. How much damage? This would depend largely on where the earthquake epicenter was located. If the quake should be centered in a sparsely populated area, property damage and

As rated on the Richter Scale, the 1971 San Fernando Valley earthquake was in the "moderate" class. Even so, property damage was very great.

loss of life would be minimal. However, a quake of magnitude 7 releases energy that is roughly equal to a blast of one million tons of TNT. This much power unleashed in the crust could do incredible damage in a densely populated region.

The 1906 San Francisco earthquake rated 8.3 on the Richter Scale. This was truly a major earthquake, for only about one quake of this magnitude takes place each year. On the other hand, the 6.6 Richter rating of the 1971 San Fernando Valley, California, temblor places this shocker in the "moderate" class. Residents of this area might take exception to the term "moderate," for transportation routes were blocked, utilities disrupted, more than 700 buildings damaged, and some 1000 landslides were triggered. Fortunately, seismologists estimate that only about twenty earthquakes of 7 or greater magnitude occur annually. This is comforting to know—especially when we consider that the earth is wracked by more than one million earthquakes each and every year.

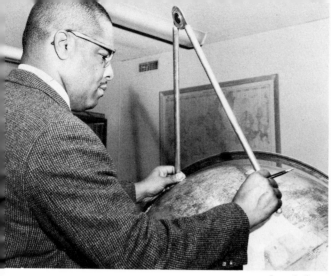

Studies made at the Environmental Science Services Administration's Earthquake Information Center may prove helpful in developing a system of earthquake prediction.

Jerry Coffman,
ESSA Earthquake Information Center

EARTHQUAKE PREDICTION

Few people—particularly geologists and Californians—express surprise when an earthquake is reported in California. This is, after all, "earthquake country" and an occasional quake is to be expected. If scientists can predict *where* earthquakes might occur, why should they not be able to forecast *when* they might strike?

Although seismologists have recognized the desirability and perhaps the possibility of an earthquake warning system, no such method has yet been developed. However, much research is being done on this problem and such a system may be in operation in the future. For example, the United States Geological Survey has elaborate arrays of recording instruments set up in California and Nevada. Changes in the established patterns of seismic activity, variations in the temperature, magnetism, and other physical properties of the underground rocks, as well as deformation of the surface rocks are continually being recorded by these devices. Hopefully, some pattern will emerge that might be used to forewarn of an impending quake.

Progress is being made and much is being learned. Even so, it will be a long time before Californians are issued "earthquake alerts" similar to those which warn of the impending onslaught of a tornado or hurricane in other parts of the country.

Chapter 9

"CHIMNEYS"
IN EARTH'S CRUST

Volcanoes, like earthquakes, are among Earth's more interesting and spectacular phenomena. Since the earliest recorded history man has viewed the trembling earth and its fiery mountains with awesome fear. And not without reason, for here is dramatic evidence of the powerful forces bottled up within the earth.

The Mexican farmer who witnessed the birth of Parícutin Volcano in his cornfield, the ancient Romans who lost their homes—and their lives—at Pompeii, and the thousands of tourists who have thrilled to the fireworks of Hawaii's Kilauea Volcano all had one thing in common: they were awed by our "stable" planet's tremendous display of power.

Superstition, legend, and mystery have always surrounded these fiery mountains. Nor is this surprising. Even in this enlightened age these mountainous "chimneys" in the earth are not fully understood. Geologists still speculate on certain problems of volcanism and many secrets are hidden in their smouldering furnaces. Indeed, some confusion even surrounds the use of the word "volcano," for it is used to describe both the eruption of earth materials and the mountain that results from the eruption.

What, then, is a volcano? Volcanoes are vents or openings in the earth's crust through which molten rock and other volcanic

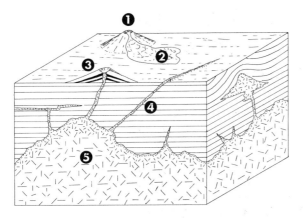

This cross-sectional view of the earth shows a cinder cone (1); a lava flow (2); a composite cone (3); an intrusive mass, or dike (4); and (5) the magma reservoir beneath the surface.

products are extruded. Volcanic eruptions are the products of the geologic process of *volcanism*—the movement of molten rock within the earth and on its surface.

There are many kinds of volcanoes, but they typically occur as cone-shaped mountains topped by a funnel-shaped crater. A conduit (or tube) passes through the cone and connects the crater with the buried magma reservoir. Some of the molten rock in the magma chamber may be intruded into the earth's crust to form intrusive or plutonic igneous rocks. But during periods of volcanic eruption, magma is released on the surface to form volcanic or extrusive igneous rocks.

VOLCANOES IN ACTION

In A.D. 79, Italy's restless Mount Vesuvius blazed into action, burying the ancient cities of Pompeii and Herculaneum beneath a suffocating blanket of cinders and volcanic ash. Centuries later —in 1902—the village of St Pierre, on the West Indies island of

National Park Service

Hawaii's Kilauea Volcano has been studied in such detail that it has been called a "pet" volcano.

Parícutin Volcano appeared quite unexpectedly in a Mexican corn field in 1943.

Field Museum of Natural History

Martinique, was wiped out by a cloud of fiery gas that blasted through the side of Mount Pelée—a so-called "peaceful slumbering" volcano. More recently, two villages in Mexico were completely buried beneath lava flows that were produced by Parícutin Volcano which unexpectedly appeared in 1943.

These now-famous volcanic eruptions not only emphasize the force and potential destruction of volcanic activity, they are evidence of the different types of materials that may be produced during an eruption. The most familiar volcanic product is molten rock called lava. Red- or white-hot when it pours from the earth, the liquid rock eventually cools to form a solid igneous rock that is also called lava. Thus, the term lava is used to describe both the liquid volcanic material as well as the solid rock produced from it. It was massive flows of molten lava that buried the Mexican villages of San Juan and Parícutin in 1944.

Volcanoes are not all alike. They differ in the cones that they build, the manner in which they erupt, and the types of material that they produce. Molten lava, for example, may differ considerably from one volcano to the next. Some lavas are thick and pasty like bread dough. Flows composed of viscous lavas plod slowly—but relentlessly—across the land. Other lavas are more fluid and give rise to faster moving lava flows. How fast? The *viscosity* (and hence, the rate of flow) of lava is determined by the chemical composition and temperature of the molten rock. Lava, like water, tends to run "downhill," so the slope of the surface on which it is flowing is also a factor. In rare cases certain Hawaiian lavas have moved at speeds of ten to twenty-five miles per hour. Other flows have moved as little as a few feet per day.

Molten lava hardens to form rocks that are equally varied. Some are riddled with holes that represent the location of former gas bubbles, one type consists of rough blocks, and yet another

The little village of San Juan was completely buried beneath a massive lava flow as a result of Parícutin Volcano's unexpected eruption in 1943. The tower of the village church serves as a "tombstone" which marks the burial site of the village.

Jennie A. Matthews

U. S. Geological Survey

This lava fall, about 100 feet high, is typical of the liquid materials thrown out during a volcanic eruption.

is characterized by relatively smooth, ropy surfaces. Obsidian, or volcanic glass, is a distinctive type of lava that cooled relatively quickly. Because it breaks with a shell-like fracture resembling that of flint, Indians used it to make knives, arrowheads, and other weapons and implements.

Strange as it may seem, most lava is not erupted through the volcano's crater. It flows, instead, from cracks which open up near the base or on the flanks of the volcanic cone. Flank eruptions of this type are especially common in the Hawaiian volcanoes.

Gaseous matter—such as that which snuffed out the lives of

some 30,000 residents of St. Pierre—is associated with most volcanic eruptions. Volcanic gases consist mostly of water vapor, with varying amounts of carbon dioxide, hydrogen sulfide, and chlorine.

Water vapor, or steam, is most abundant, for it is the major force behind volcanic eruptions. When water passes from a liquid to gaseous state its volume is increased by about one thousand. This rapid expansion of great quantities of water can give rise to incredibly powerful explosions. When an eruption occurs, escaping gases often become mixed with small solid particles of volcanic dust and ash. These produce the dense, so-called clouds of "smoke" that accompany certain eruptions. This is not actually smoke, however, for this gas is not the direct product of combustion.

A variety of solid materials may be thrown out during volcanic eruptions. This is especially true of those volcanoes which erupt more or less violently. Known as *pyroclastic* ("fire-broken") materials, these volcanic igneous rocks range from fine dust to boulders the size of a house. The area surrounding the volcano

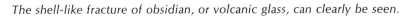

The shell-like fracture of obsidian, or volcanic glass, can clearly be seen.

Jennie A. Matthews

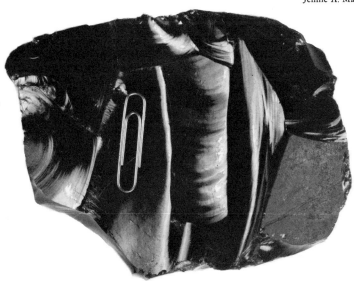

Solid material like this volcanic bomb is produced by the more explosive eruptions.

may also be pelted with volcanic bombs. Spherical or pear-shaped objects, the bombs form from large masses of lava that harden as they swirl through the air. Cinders, ash, and small pebble-sized fragments of hardened lava may also be produced. Pumice—a glassy, spongelike pyroclastic filled with countless small holes—is a solid product that is generated during certain more explosive volcanic eruptions. Mount Vesuvius has produced much pyroclastic material and some of this volcanic debris was responsible for the destruction of Pompeii.

FUEL FOR THE FURNACE

The fiery eruptions and thunderous explosions that characterize many volcanic eruptions have fascinated—and frightened—man since the dawn of time. This is reflected in the very word "volcano," for it comes from the Latin words *vulcanus* or *volcanus*. This term was applied to volcanoes because of the Italian island of Vulcano which the ancients believed to be inhabited by Vulcan, the Roman god of fire. Vulcan was also believed to be the blacksmith for all the other gods. Vulcan's shop was assumed to be in the volcanic cone that formed the island of Vulcano.

The smoke from Vulcano's eruptions was thought to be coming from Vulcan's forge, and the rumblings and vibrations within the cone must have been produced as the mighty blacksmith pounded his anvil.

Even now earth scientists are not sure how Earth's furnaces are fired, but they do know that intense heat is needed to melt solid rock and trigger a volcanic eruption. Volcanologists also agree that the melting of rock takes place rather deep within the earth. This most likely occurs in the upper mantle or the lower part of the crust where temperatures are high and pressures are very great. It has been suggested, for example, that since earth temperatures rise steadily with increasing depth, the more deeply buried rocks are likely to be in a molten state. Curiously enough, there is reason to believe that these deeply buried rocks actually remain in the solid state as long as they are under pressure. However, in areas where there are breaks in the crust, the confining pressures are released, permitting the rock to liquify as pressures are diminished.

Another theory assumes a heat source produced by high temperatures generated from friction that accompanies rock deformation during crustal movements. When rock masses break, fold, and slide over one another much frictional heat is produced. Supporters of this idea point out that areas of volcanic activity are closely associated with regions of recent crustal deformation and mountain-building movements. They note also that the distribution of volcanoes is not random, but concentrated in well-defined belts that approximate the distribution of earthquakes. Most volcanoes are near the sea and in areas where rock fracturing may have occurred. The "Pacific Ring of Fire," the volcanic band that borders the Pacific Ocean, contains most of the world's active volcanoes. Another large concentration of volcanoes is in the Mediterranean Zone which circles the globe roughly parallel to the equator. However, a few volcanoes are scattered in the

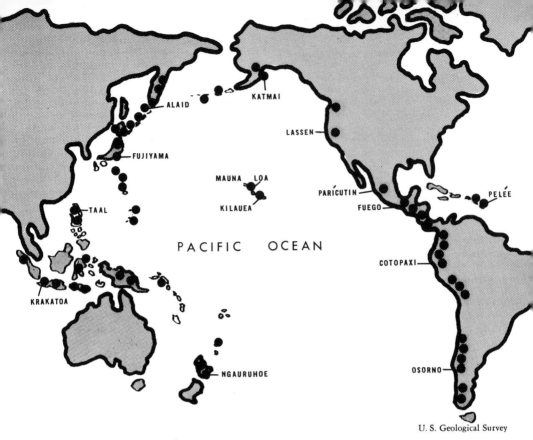

Map showing distribution of major areas of volcanic activity.

interiors of the continents.

Some geologists think that "hot pockets" within the earth are caused by localized concentrations of radioactive minerals. It is assumed that these radioactive products are capable of generating sufficient heat to melt the rocks surrounding them. These, in turn, would provide the magma for the volcanic eruption. Despite these "educated guesses," science has not yet determined the origin of Earth's internal heat or what triggers a volcanic eruption. It is generally assumed, however, that the causes of volcanic activity are produced by the same internal forces that cause earthquakes, metamorphism, and mountain-building uplifts.

VOLCANOES SHAPE THE LAND

Few people have ever seen a volcano in action, but most of us have seen evidence of how volcanism has molded the landscape.

Washington's Mount Rainier, the "lunar landscape" of Craters of the Moon National Monument in Idaho, and Oregon's Crater Lake appear to have little in common. But the geologist knows that these areas were quite literally "born of fire," for they are all evidence of how volcanic eruptions have shaped the land.

Each volcano has its own particular "style" of eruption and each type of eruption produces different kinds of land forms. Volcanic mountains such as Mount Rainier, Japan's Mount Fuji-yama, and Mount Shasta in California are literally sprinkled across Earth's face. These are among the more spectacular and important volcanic land forms and will be discussed in a later chapter on mountains and mountain-building.

Although the typical volcanic eruption produces some form of volcanic mountain, other land forms may also be created. For example, *fissure*, or *Icelandic*, eruptions produce massive land forms known as *lava plateaus*. During a fissure eruption torrents of lava pour out of cracks in the earth's crust. These floods of molten rock pile one lava flow atop the other until many thousands of square miles may be blanketed with hundreds of feet of solidified lava. The Columbia River Plateau of Oregon, Washington, Nevada, and Idaho is a major land feature that was formed in this way.

Oregon's Crater Lake is one of our most popular national parks. It is also evidence of another type of volcanic land form, the *caldera*. These nearly circular, basin-shaped depressions occur in the tops of volcanoes, but are usually much larger than craters. Some calderas originate when the top of a volcano collapses or literally falls in. Others are formed when the top of the mountain is blasted away during a violent eruption. Some, like the depression filled by Crater Lake, were produced by the combined forces of collapse and explosion. The caldera occupied by Crater Lake probably formed about 6000 years ago. It was then that Mount Mazama—a vanished 12,000-foot volcanic peak —was rocked by a series of shattering explosions that ripped out

Oregon's famous Crater Lake occupies a caldera formed when an ancient volcanic cone collapsed. There is evidence that some of the moon's craters may have been formed as similar collapse structures.

much of Mazama's interior. As the lava drained from beneath the volcano, there was weakening in the upper part of the cone. Deprived of support by the underlying material, the bulk of Mount Mazama eventually collapsed under its own weight.

The newly-formed caldera gradually filled with water, forming a lake that covers about twenty square miles and is almost 2000 feet deep. Whether old Mazama "blew its top" or simply "fell in" is not known for sure. But one thing is certain: the volcano did not die easily. Within the last thousand years new vents apparently opened up on the caldera floor. These eruptions must have been explosive, for they produced at least three cinder cones. One of these is Wizard Island, a symmetrical mound of ash and cinder which can be seen in the lake today.

SOME VOLCANIC SIDE EFFECTS

The effects of volcanism are not limited to volcanoes alone. In some areas of past and present volcanic activity, steam, volcanic gases, and hot water are escaping from the earth. *Fumaroles* are cracks through which steam and gas escape, and *hot springs* contain waters that derive their heat from hot subsurface rocks. *Geysers* are special types of hot springs that intermittently erupt a column of steam and hot water. Some geysers, such as Yellowstone National Park's Old Faithful, erupt with remarkable regularity. However, most geysers perform quite erratically.

Jennie A. Matthews

Geysers such as the one seen here in Yellowstone National Park derive their heat from hot subsurface rocks. The hot groundwater has deposited a cone of mineral material around the geyser's opening.

CAN ERUPTIONS BE PREDICTED?

Some volcanoes, like Kilauea in Hawaii, are said to be *active* volcanoes. They are continually or periodically in a state of eruption. A volcano that is now inactive, but that has erupted within modern times is classed as *dormant*. Mount Vesuvius in Italy is a dormant, or "sleeping," volcano that erupted after centuries of inactivity. Those volcanoes that are not known to have erupted in historic times are said to be *extinct*. Nature, however, does not always abide by man-made classifications such as active, dormant, and extinct. Lassen Peak, a so-called "extinct" volcano in California suddenly came to life in 1914 and was in eruption for almost seven years. Lassen Peak is now classified as an active volcano.

Although active volcanoes must be considered capable of eruption at any time, it would be helpful to know approximately when they might erupt. Volcanologists are literally studying volcanoes inside and out as they search for geologic clues as to when they may erupt and what pattern the eruption might follow.

A long-time study of certain active volcanoes reveals that many of them have rather characteristic and well-defined patterns of activity. For example, Mount Etna, Mount Vesuvius, and Kilauea Volcano appear to have eruption cycles that are somewhat predictable. When cyclical patterns of eruptions can be established, this provides a clue as to when the volcano might erupt, as well as the sequence of events in the eruption.

The seismograph has been an especially useful tool, because a series of earthquakes near an active volcano may indicate that "fireworks" are in the offing. The *tiltmeter*, an instrument that measures variations in the tilting of the volcano's summit, can

Chester Mullen, National Park Service

Lassen Peak, the only active volcano in the continental United States, is seen here erupting on October 6, 1915.

U. S. Geological Survey

Vulcanologists keep constant watch at Kilauea Volcano for telltale signs that might warn of an impending eruption. The seismographs on the left may detect earth tremors resulting from the movement of magma beneath the mountain.

also warn of a forthcoming eruption. Before a volcano erupts, magma begins to rise under the volcano and localizes a few miles beneath the surface. As pressures and temperatures soar, the magma expands, pushing the overlying rocks upward and aside. This literally causes the volcano to expand or swell and these changes caused by the inflating mountains will be detected by the tiltmeter.

Other instruments may detect changes in the earth's magnetism which are caused by the subsurface movement of magma. Infrared photographs are also taken to determine if there are telltale "hot spots" that might warn of an impending eruption.

Volcanologists have learned much about the events and evidence that warn that a volcano *might* erupt. But is not yet possible to make accurate eruption predictions for even the most-studied volcano.

Chapter 10

THE RIDDLE OF THE CONTINENTS

Two hundred million years ago New York was located at the equator and the present-day east coast of the United States trended in an east-wide direction. The Atlantic Ocean? It barely existed—if at all—for the North American continent is believed to have been joined with South America and Africa.

Science fiction? Not if we are properly reading the record in the rocks. There is steadily mounting evidence that this was the global geography at one time in the geologic past.

CONTINENTAL RAFTS

Early geologists quite naturally assumed that the continents were stable and unmoving. There was no reason to believe that the shape and position of the lands and seas had not always been as we see them today.

Now we are not so sure. Consider, for example, the observations of Sir Francis Bacon. As early as 1620, this famous English philosopher noted the remarkable resemblance of the Atlantic coasts of Africa and South America. And in 1658, François Placet published a work in which he stated that " . . . prior to the Flood, America was not separated from the rest of the world."

Two centuries later, Antonio Snider also commented on the matching outlines of Africa and South America. But more important, he noted a distinct resemblance between species of fossil plants that occurred in both Europe and America. Then in 1885, Edward Suess, an Austrian geologist, uncovered additional clues in the continental mystery. As he studied scattered continental rocks in the Southern Hemisphere, he learned that they had many features in common. Using this evidence, Suess fitted the pieces of his "continental jigsaw puzzle" together. The result? One monstrous landmass that he christened Gondwanaland.

Bacon, Plaçet, Snider, and Suess made valuable observations and gathered geologic evidence which strongly suggested that the continents have not always been as they are today. It remained, however, for Alfred Wegener (a German meteorologist) to attempt an explanation of this remarkable phenomenon. His solution—the *theory of continental drift*—was proposed in 1912 and triggered a scientific controversy that has raged for decades.

Briefly stated, Wegener—like Suess—proposed the earlier existence of a single ancestral continent which he named Pangea (meaning "all-earth"). Wegener assumed that his "mother" continent broke apart some 200 million years ago and the fragments slowly drifted to their present locations. In addition to earlier evidence, he used rocks, fossils, and other geologic clues to support his controversial idea. Despite great differences today, Wegener contended that world-wide climates, global geography, and the distribution of life forms had once been similar in different parts of the globe. Was it not logical, then, to assume that the now widely separated continents were once much closer—perhaps even linked—to one another?

The battle was soon joined as "Drifters" and "Anti-drifters" heatedly debated this apparently outlandish proposal. Pros and cons—both valid and invalid—were put forth by both sides. But the supporters of the theory were hard put to explain the basic objection: How, when, and why did Pangea split apart? Nor

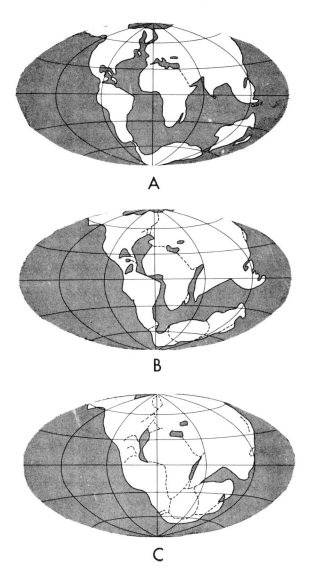

A

B

C

The theory of continental drift assumes that the present continents resulted from the breaking apart of a supercontinent that existed during Late Paleozoic time. At (A) the earth is seen as it might have appeared 600,000 years ago during Pleistocene time; during the Tertiary Period, about 70 million years ago the continents were arranged as shown at (B). The map (C) shows the continents joined together as they might have been during Late Paleozoic time, some 270 million years ago.

could the "Drifters" come up with a satisfactory mechanism capable of sliding whole continents thousands of miles apart. The "Anti-drifters," on the other hand, lacked evidence to prove that the continents could *not* drift. And so, as the debaters reached a stalemate, continental drift was ignored or ridiculed as earth scientists turned to more pressing problems.

Today Wegener's proposal has been removed from the mothballs and has far more friends than foes. It is true that his "mother" continent, Pangea, has been replaced by two supercontinents: Laurasia in the Northern Hemisphere and Gondwanaland in the Southern Hemisphere. Believers in two-continent theory drift say that Eurasia and North America formed Laurasia. Gondwanaland consisted of Antarctic, Australia, Africa, South America, Malagasy, the Indian subcontinent, and various submerged fragments.

Many earth scientists find this once-revolutionary theory quite logical in the light of recent scientific discoveries. These show that the continents have not only shifted in the past, they are drifting even now. It has been learned, for example, that Iceland is being separated by the same forces that are thought to drift continents. An English scientist has found that parts of Iceland are being pulled apart at the rate of one-third inch per year.

The "Drifters" have gathered supporting testimony from many sources. Paleontologists cite the distribution and evolution of certain plant and animal fossils as evidence that they developed on a continuous continental landmass. Geochemical studies reveal striking similarities between the chemical characteristics of rocks of the ocean floor and those on the margins of opposing continents. Geochronologists have obtained radiometric dates that suggest a common age for rocks in such scattered places as Africa, South America, India, and Australia. Some of these rocks have, moreover, been subjected to the same geologic processes during the same part of geologic history. In short, there is mounting reason to believe that the matching rock sections in these widely scattered areas were once more or less continuous, uninterrupted landmasses.

SPREADING SEA FLOORS AND WANDERING POLES

Curiously enough, some of the strongest evidence in favor of drifting land has been found on the bottom of the sea. Marine geologists studying the *oceanic ridges* have found this 40,000-mile-long submarine mountain chain to be the source of much valuable scientific information. This is especially true of the Mid-Atlantic Ridge. This 10,000-mile undersea range begins at the southern tip of Africa and snakes its way across the ocean floor to Iceland. It averages twenty miles in width and its rocky spine rises as much as a mile above the ocean floor.

The rocks on and near the Mid-Atlantic Ridge tell us much about the crust and how the continents may have drifted. Investigations reveal that the ocean floor near the ridge is not stationary, but, like the continents, is spreading apart. A deep rift, or trench, runs along the crest of the Mid-Atlantic Ridge. The expansion of the sea bottom appears to be associated with volcanic activity that originates beneath the ridge. Molten rock periodically boils out of the ridge's central rift and lava flows down the flanks of the submarine range. Each time there is an eruption, the pressure of the outpouring lava pushes the sides of the trench progressively farther apart. The newer lava hardens in and adjacent to the central rift. Consequently, the flows of lava become increasingly older on each side of the trench. The result is a series of progressively older parallel bands of lava.

What tells us that the rocks are increasingly older on each side of the Mid-Atlantic Ridge? The clues are found in tiny "fossil" magnets embedded in the lava flows. Most of us have seen how Earth's magnetic poles cause the needle of a compass to line up in a north-south direction. When rocks containing

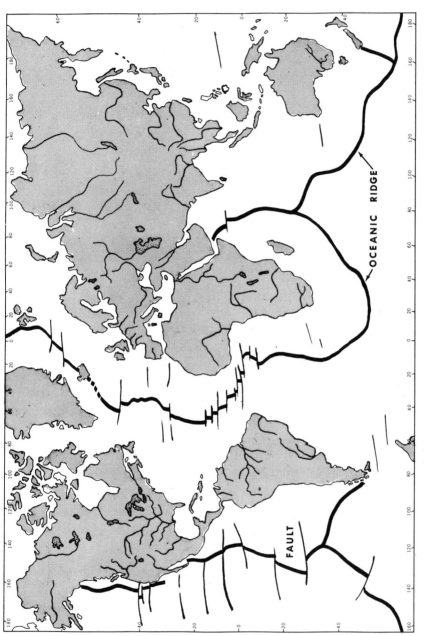

The oceanic ridges form a great submarine mountain chain about 40,000 miles long. In many places they are offset by large transform faults.

tiny particles of magnetic iron minerals were formed, the flecks of iron tended to line up with the earth's magnetic field as it was when the rocks were formed. Equally important, these tiny "compass needles" retain their magnetic properties for hundreds of millions of years. This rock characteristic is called *paleomagnetism*, a word that literally means "ancient magnetism."

In rocks of any given age, the "fossil compasses" are in line with the magnetic poles as they were at the time of the rocks' origin. But in older or younger rocks, the telltale "needles" may point in quite different directions—evidence that the poles had changed. In both instances, however, paleomagnetism might indicate polar directions unlike the north and south of today. Paleomagnetic studies suggest that there have been many changes in the earth's magnetic field. Indeed, they reveal that the poles have done quite a bit of wandering and that Earth's magnetic field may have been completely reversed at least nine times in the last $3\frac{1}{2}$ billion years!

Scientists have plotted curves to indicate the position of the poles during various chapters in earth history. They consider these to be evidence of continental drift, because their studies yield different polar curves for different continents. If the continents have *not* drifted, it is assumed that the polar curves for all continents would remain the same.

The "fossil magnets" in the lava flows on either side of the Mid-Atlantic Ridge are of interest to students of sea floor spreading and continental drift. They indicate that one flow will have normal polarity while the next shows that the poles have been reversed. This suggests that one lava flow occurred when our magnetic poles were much as they are today. However, the next band of lava was deposited many thousands of years later when the poles were reversed. As a result of continuing lava flows and changing poles, the growth of the ocean floor has been recorded in a series of magnetized bands of normal and reversed

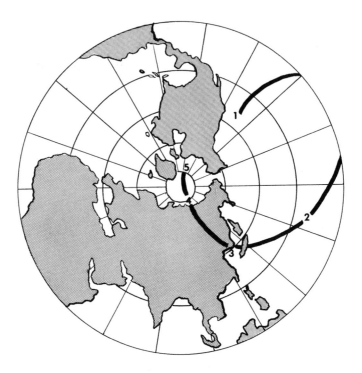

As indicated by the numbers, the earth's magnetic pole has been at different places during different parts of geologic time.

polarity. The stripelike pattern of these alternating bands records the development of the sea bottom much as the rings in a tree trunk reveal the growth pattern of a tree.

As the sea floor expands, countless fractures develop in the relatively thin, brittle rocks of the oceanic crust. Many of these fractures have a lateral (sideways) movement and are called *transform faults*. The lava flows, paleomagnetism, and the transform faults suggest that the sea floor is continually tearing apart and being repaired by lava flowing from the central trench.

Some scientists have suggested that the expanding sea bottom is somewhat like a great conveyor belt. In other words, as the ocean bottom spreads, it may be carrying the continents along with it.

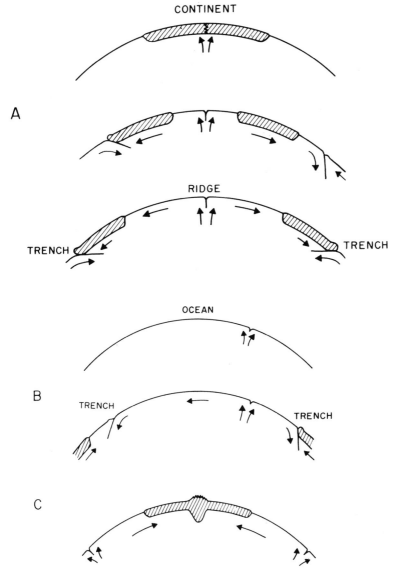

CONTINENT

A

RIDGE

TRENCH

TRENCH

OCEAN

B

TRENCH

TRENCH

C

Fred Vine, *Journal of Geological Education*

The process of sea floor spreading appears to play a vital role in continental drift and plate tectonics. Diagrams (A) and (B) illustrate the stages and possible configurations that might result from rifting and spreading beneath the continental and oceanic crust, respectively. Diagram (C) illustrates the possibility of two continental blocks coming together over a downcurrent.

PLATE TECTONICS—AN EXPLANATION?

Recent advances in geophysical research have provided the "Drifters" with still more support. The recently proposed theory of *plate tectonics* (or *global tectonics*) is gathering support from many earth scientists and looks most promising. Hopefully, this new concept may provide answers to some of the more troublesome questions surrounding continental drift, polar wandering, sea floor spreading, earthquake belts, and certain mountain-building processes.

Although too complex for a detailed discussion, the theory of plate tectonics generally assumes that the earth has an outer "shell" which is composed of the crust and the upper part of the mantle. This shell is fifty to sixty miles thick and rests on another part of the mantle called the *asthenosphere*. Approximately 400 miles thick, the asthenosphere is made of rock material that is hot, soft, and relatively weak. Equally important, this part of the mantle has little strength and will flow in response to motions of the outer shell.

It has been suggested that Earth's outer shell can be divided into six major rigid plates. In addition to material from the upper mantle, these massive slabs contain both oceanic and continental crust and move on the asthenosphere much as ice floes float on water. The six plates of shell material are thought to be as much as sixty miles thick. Between them they carry the continents and continental shelves of the ocean floor. There are also several smaller slabs, and all plates—large and small—have changed size and shape over the ages.

Throughout geologic time, the raftlike plates have moved over the earth's surface, and their cargo of continents and marine sediments with them. Where plates move apart beneath the sea, an oceanic ridge is formed. Lava rises from the mantle, flows out of the central rift, and new material is added to the plate. Plates grinding against each other may produce fractures respon-

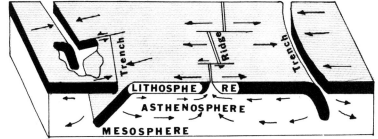

U. S. Geological Survey after Isacks, Oliver, and Sykes, 1968

This idealized cross-section shows the probable nature of contacts between tectonic plates. The arrow indicates relative movements and the asthenosphere can be seen just beneath the crust or lithosphere.

sible for the ridge's transform faults. Plate movement might also be the cause of certain earthquakes. For example, Alaska's destructive Good Friday earthquake of 1964, may have been caused by underthrusting of the Pacific plate at the Aleutians.

As two plates move toward each other, they may be compressed and shortened to form a folded mountain belt (see Chapter 11). When two plates collide, the edge of one slab is bent downward and forced below into the asthenosphere. There it is heated and absorbed into the mantle.

The movement of continent-sized rafts and entire ocean bottoms requires a most powerful and competent mechanism. Although the force that drives tectonic plates is not completely understood, mantle circulation by convection currents has been proposed. As we shall see in the next chapter, these circulating heat cells are apparently capable of generating powerful forces. It has also been suggested that the sinking part of the plate, which is denser than the hotter surrounding material, pulls the rest of the plate down with it.

Will plate tectonics be the key to the solution of the geological mysteries described in this chapter? The theory has created great excitement in geologic circles and has opened up many new avenues of research. From a more practical standpoint it may

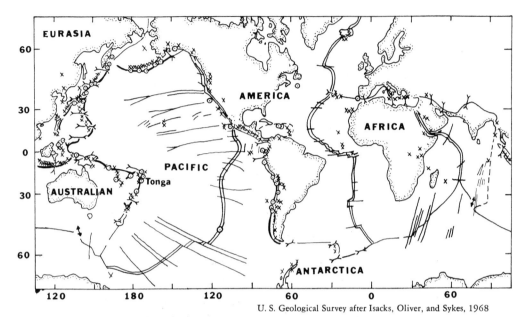

U. S. Geological Survey after Isacks, Oliver, and Sykes, 1968

The concept of global (or plate) tectonics assumes the presence of six major tectonic plates (Eurasia, Australian, Pacific, America, Africa, and Anarctica). The mid-ocean ridges and transform faults can be seen where they appear in the ocean basins. Active volcanoes are indicated by X and open circles represent earthquakes that generated tsunamis.

even be of help in locating valuable ore deposits and oil fields. Application of plate theory also offers some promise in developing methods of earthquake prediction. Meanwhile, much remains to be learned about global tectonics and only the tests of time and research will prove its scientific merit.

Chapter 11

THE MYSTERY OF MOUNTAINS

The mystery and magnificance of mountains have always had a special attraction for man. In primitive times they were believed to be the home of the gods—towering perches from which the deities could supervise the earth. Even now, Alaska's 20,320-foot Mount McKinley—our continent's highest mountain—is frequently called Denali, "The High One." This name, coined by early Indians, typifies the reverence and awe that still surround many of our planet's more lofty peaks. Mountains have also provided some of the world's most spectacular scenery.

Yet like so many of Earth's more obvious features and processes, mountains and mountain-building remain among Earth's more intriguing mysteries. What, for example, *is* a mountain? The term is strictly relative, for one man's mountain is another man's hill—and vice versa. Consider the Black Hills of South Dakota. These typical dome mountains are called "hills" despite the fact that their highest peak looms nearly 2000 feet higher than Maine's Mount Katahdin. If height is not the key to the "mountain vs. hill" puzzle, will the shape, structure, or nature of the rocks provide the answer? Generally speaking, the term "mountain" has been applied to countless land forms that rise prominently above the surrounding landscape. But geologically speaking, the term is more properly applied in light of what is known about the origin and development of the elevated land form.

Ginny Wood, Camp Denali, College, Alaska

Alaska's 20,320-foot Mount McKinley is North America's highest mountain. The hikers are resting at the foot of a glacier.

Although referred to as "hills," the Black Hills of South Dakota are considerably higher than many land forms designated as mountains. The famous "stone faces" on Mount Rushmore have been carved out of ancient granite that formed the core of these typical dome mountains.

Jennie A. Matthews

VOLCANOES AS MOUNTAINS

We have already seen that volcanoes differ in a number of ways. But regardless of what or how they erupt, each builds its own particular type of land form.

Volcanoes that erupt violently construct *cinder cones* or *explosive cones* around their vents. Consisting mostly of pyroclastic material such as cinders and ashes, cones of this sort usually have very steep sides. They seldom are more than 1000 feet high and may be the result of a single volcanic explosion. Sunset Crater in Arizona and New Mexico's Capulin Mountain are typical cinder cones.

Cones composed of alternating layers of lava and cinders and ash are called *stratovolcanoes*, or *composite cones*. Volcanoes that build mountains of this type have alternating periods of explosive and relatively quiet eruptions. Lava is discharged during the less violent eruptions and the layers of cinders and ash are blown out during phases of explosive activity. Italy's Mount Vesuvius, Mount Rainier in Washington, and Mount Fujiyama are well-known examples of stratovolcanoes.

The Hawaiian volcanoes are noted for their rather quiet eruptions during which immense quantities of lava may be discharged. Hawaiian eruptions produce mountains called *lava domes*, or *shield volcanoes*, consisting of countless overlapping lava flows piled one upon the other. These broad, rounded mountains have gently sloping sides and may cover hundreds of square miles. Mauna Loa, Mauna Kea, and Kilauea are Hawaiian volcanoes of this type.

Volcanic mountains are numerous around the margin of the Pacific Ocean and include the Cascade Range of Oregon and Washington. Here can be found volcanic features such as Mount Rainier, Mount Hood, and Crater Lake's caldera. Another belt of "fire-born" mountains trends eastward from southeastern Europe through the Mediterranean and southern Asia. The

Explosions from Cerro Negro Volcano in west-central Nicaragua have thrown out ash and cinder that formed a symmetrical cinder cone. Lava flows from flank eruptions can be seen near the base of the cone.

Jennie A. Matthews

Glacier-covered Mount Rainier is a typical example of a stratovolcano or composite cone.

Mauna Loa Volcano on the island of Hawaii has the low, rounded profile of a typical shield volcano.

Gordon A. Macdonald

oceanic ridges are also submarine volcanic ranges. The distribution of volcanic mountains suggests that their origin is connected with deep faults that extend through the earth's crust to the mantle. Localized pockets of magma in the upper part of the mantle or lower part of the crust provide the materials from which the mountain is built.

DOME MOUNTAINS—"BLISTERS" ON THE CRUST

Mountains of volcanic origin are generally easily recognized because of their composition and characteristic shapes. The processes that elevate other mountains are not always so easily determined. *Dome mountains*, for example, may be produced by the same type of lateral compression that produces folded or more complex mountain ranges (see page 114). Other dome mountains, however, appear to be caused by a mass of molten rock material intruded into the overlying sedimentary rocks. As the hot magma moved toward the surface, the rocks above it were arched upward, producing a blister-like bulge.

Mountains produced by doming are usually roughly circular in outline and the more resistant—typically igneous—rocks lie in the center. The overlying sedimentary rocks have been stripped away by erosion, and their remnants slope away from the central region in all directions. The Black Hills of South Dakota, the Adirondacks of northern New York, and Utah's Henry Mountains are typical examples of dome mountains.

SHIFTING CRUSTAL BLOCKS

Carved from a gigantic crustal block that is more than four hundred miles long and as much as eighty miles wide, the Sierra Nevada is one of the world's great mountain ranges. This single, tilted block forms an unbroken mountain chain almost as extensive as the combined Swiss, French, and Italian Alps.

The rock record clearly indicates that the Sierra Nevada block

A typical fault block mountain range, the Tetons were developed along the Teton Fault (dotted line). Glacial deposits have developed at the base of the range and in the foreground.

was produced by faulting. This vertical movement tore the great crustal fragment loose and tilted it toward the west. The sharp eastern edge of the block rises more than two miles above sea level. The western margin of the Sierra Nevada block lies nearly five miles beneath the surface of the Pacific Ocean.

The Teton Range of Wyoming is another typical *fault block mountain* range. The block from which the Tetons is formed also has a short steep slope on one side and a longer, more gentle slope on the other. Neither the Tetons or the Sierra Nevada has retained the blocklike shape that their name implies. Instead, their once-level surfaces have been carved into a series of sharp, rugged peaks. These finishing touches to the landscape were provided by glacial erosion and weathering.

"LEFTOVER" MOUNTAINS

The Catskills of New York are rather subdued when compared to such spectacular ranges as the Cascades and Sierra Nevada. Yet these elevated land forms are another type of mountain. The Catskills, like the Cumberland Mountains of the eastern United States, consist of rocks that have not been greatly disturbed or deformed. Known as *residual, dissected,* or *erosional mountains,* these "leftover" land forms are underlain by thick piles of essentially flat-lying rocks. Each of these mountainous regions was once an extensive, flat-surfaced plateau that was subjected to gentle uplift. However, the original level surface has been carved into mountainous terrain by stream erosion.

WRINKLES IN EARTH'S CRUST

It may be difficult to imagine, but on some parts of the continents, the rocks have literally been crumpled into a series of great wrinkle-like folds. Indeed, Earth's mightiest mountain ranges have been formed from the rumpling of massive piles of sedimentary rocks that were originally in a horizontal position.

As mentioned earlier, some of the more baffling geological puzzles center around the "hows" and "whys" of mountain-building. This is especially true of *folded mountains,* for the internal forces behind the process of folding are not clearly understood. Proof of rock-folding is quite obvious in ranges such as the Appalachians, Alps, and Rocky Mountains. Here folds which originated deep within the earth now lie many thousands of feet above sea level. How could solid crustal rocks bend and buckle to form these folds? And why do most folded mountain ranges consist of great thicknesses of sedimentary rock that may contain fossilized sea plants and animals? Equally baffling is where such

The sedimentary rocks in this mountain range have been crumpled up into a series of tight folds.

thick layers of ocean sediment were deposited and how these prehistoric sea floors were elevated.

In an attempt to solve these mysteries geological detectives have done some scientific sleuthing in many of the world's folded mountain ranges. The clues they have gathered tell the following story. The ocean sediments and marine organisms were originally deposited on the bottoms of elongated, ocean-filled troughs. Known as *geosynclines,* these great troughs received their sediment as streams poured sand, silt, and gravel into the ancient seaway. Then, as now, countless plants and animals inhabited the oceans. When these organisms died, their remains fell to the ocean floor and were mixed with the other sediments.

Hundreds of thousands—even millions—of years passed. More organisms died, sediments were continually added, and great pressures were exerted on the more deeply buried rock particles. Eventually the sediment was tightly compressed and cemented together and marine sedimentary rocks were formed. The force

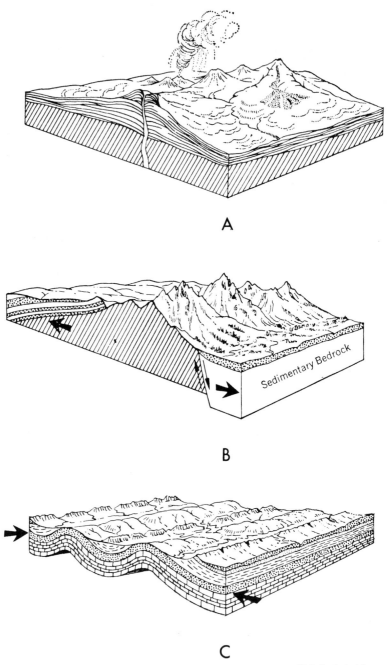

A

B

Sedimentary Bedrock

C

These cross-sections of the earth's crust show volcanic mountains (A); fault block mountains (B); and folded mountains (C).

exerted by the overlying rocks was slow but continuous. Pressures continued to mount until the deeply buried rock particles reached a state in which they were actually squeezed along in a plastic or semisolid condition. Rocks subjected to this "plastic flow" would bend or fold instead of breaking.

Time passed and still more sediments and sedimentary rocks piled up in the trough. The added weight caused the floor of the geosyncline to sag downward, deepening the trough and making room for still more sediment. In some areas as much as thirty-five miles of sediment accumulated on the bottoms of these ancient seaways.

Our geological detectives have now accounted for the origin of the fossiliferous sedimentary rocks. The conditions under which the rocks bent or flowed have also been fairly well established. But the most puzzling—and essentially unsolved—mystery remains: What great driving force lifted the folded, marine rocks thousands of feet above sea level?

Earth scientists have developed several theories or hypotheses in an attempt to explain deformation and uplift. Much study and research is behind each of these explanations, but they have not yet been proved. We might say that they are scientific guesses, that might later be established as fact.

The principle of *isostasy* has been used to explain certain types of uplift in the crust. This idea assumes that areas of the crust that are loaded with sediment will gradually sink. Conversely, those areas from which the sediments are eroded will be relieved of their burden and tend to rise. This concept helps to explain how geosynclines are warped downward. Perhaps more important, isostatic equilibrium is seen as the very delicate balance that keeps the oceans from filling up and the land from being completely eroded away.

Many early geologists supported the *contraction theory*. The earth, they said, is cooling from its original molten condition.

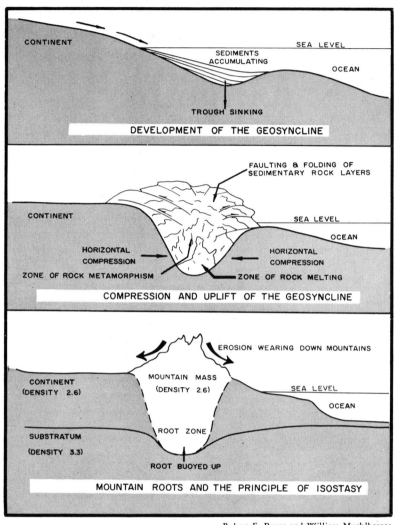

CONTINENT   SEA LEVEL
SEDIMENTS
ACCUMULATING
OCEAN

TROUGH SINKING

DEVELOPMENT OF THE GEOSYNCLINE

FAULTING & FOLDING OF
SEDIMENTARY ROCK LAYERS

CONTINENT   SEA LEVEL
OCEAN

HORIZONTAL
COMPRESSION   HORIZONTAL
COMPRESSION

ZONE OF ROCK METAMORPHISM   ZONE OF ROCK MELTING

COMPRESSION AND UPLIFT OF THE GEOSYNCLINE

EROSION WEARING DOWN MOUNTAINS

CONTINENT   MOUNTAIN MASS
(DENSITY 2.6)   (DENSITY 2.6)   SEA LEVEL
OCEAN

SUBSTRATUM
(DENSITY 3.3)   ROOT ZONE

ROOT BUOYED UP

MOUNTAIN ROOTS AND THE PRINCIPLE OF ISOSTASY

Robert E. Boyer and William Muehlberger,
Science and Children

Three stages in the development of folded mountains as explained by the geosynclinal theory.

The wrinkles in the crust—like the wrinkles on a cold, baked apple—were formed as the young planet cooled and slowly contracted.

Other geologists proposed an expanding earth. Instead of cooling and shrinking, the earth was assumed to have once been about half its present size. According to the *expansion theory* the earth was originally uniformly covered by the continental crust. As time passed and the earth expanded, the crust was broken into blocks. Continued expansion pushed the crustal blocks farther apart, and the space between them became the ocean basins. When the solid crustal blocks moved over the mantle the rocks were heated by friction. The heated, somewhat plastic rocks, were partially dragged along and rumpled into a series of folds.

Serious objections have been raised against either a shrinking or swelling earth and they have little support today. Much more popular is the *convection theory* which assumes thermal convection currents in the earth. These convection cells generate rising subsurface movements that tend to push the mountains upward.

Perhaps you have seen the convection process in boiling water. Boiling water is constantly moving. When heat is applied to the cooler water, that part sinks because it is more dense than the heated portion. This pushes up the heated water which loses its heat as it reaches the surface. The surface water then cools, becomes more dense, and settles back toward the bottom. These currents—one rising and one sinking—make up a convection cell.

It has been suggested that radioactive heating might set up convection cells in the mantle. Like boiling water in a pot, heated material would rise within the mantle. Then, as the currents cooled and turned downward, they would wrinkle the overlying crustal rocks into piles of folded rocks. Pressures exerted by the convection currents might also cause parts of the crust to move away from each other. These horizontal movements would produce drag that might crinkle and fold certain parts of the crust.

Within recent years, earth scientists interested in continental drift and sea floor spreading have come up with the concept of *plate tectonics*. And, as mentioned in the preceding chapter, their findings have provided valuable clues to the mountain-folding mechanism. It seems strange that the fundamental answers about the formation of mountain belts may eventually be discovered on the ocean floor. But considering that almost 71 per cent of the earth's surface is covered by water and only about 29 per cent is exposed on land, this may not be as strange as it would seem.

How can plate tectonics account for the world's great mountain ranges? Recent studies suggest that plate movement can cause mountain-building in two ways. One way is when a plate that has nothing but an ocean above it sinks into a trench. This can happen at the margin of a continent or at the edge of an island arc such as those around the western Pacific Ocean. The Andes of South America are believed to have formed in this way, where the Pacific plate is plunging under the American plate, creating the Peru-Chile trench.

The second way occurs when a plate carrying a continent descends into a trench and collides with an island arc or with another continent. Such a "continental crunch" may have produced the world's highest continental mountain, 29,141-foot Mount Everest. This peak, like the rest of the Himalaya Mountains, is thought to have been formed by the collision of the Indian subcontinent with Asia.

As more is learned about the theory of plate tectonics, it is becoming increasingly popular with geologists. In fact, many earth scientists see this mechanism as a unifying explanation to explain many of the more puzzling processes of continental rock deformation.

Chapter 12

OUR CHANGED
AND CHANGING EARTH

A mud-red stream slices its way across Arizona, carrying silt and sand picked up as the river carves its canyon.

In a burial ground in Massachusetts a tourist stoops to read a tombstone, its message all but erased by the slow work of the weather.

The captain of a Great Lakes ore boat steers his ship across Lake Superior, but does not associate this lake with the Ice Age glaciers that scooped out its basin.

In Peru an earthquake triggers a massive avalanche and 20,000 villagers are buried beneath countless tons of rock.

Running water, weathering, glacial ice, and landslides. These geologic tools—working individually and together—represent but a few of the ways in which the face of the earth is shaped. Land-shaping tools—more properly called *geologic agents*—are many and varied. Many work so slowly as to be imperceptible. A few strike with the deadly speed of lightning. But regardless of which tool Nature is using or how fast it works, the end result is invariably the same: change.

Fred Harvey

Running water—the greatest of all geologic agents—has carved the Grand Canyon of the Colorado River within relatively recent geologic time.

Earth has changed in the past, it is changing as you read this, and—hopefully—it will continue to change. Why "hopefully?" In this chapter we shall see that geologic change occurs in many ways. More important, we shall see how these changes affect man and his environment—for better as well as for worse.

WATER—THE MASTER TOOL

Like many commonplace objects, water is usually taken for granted, but few things are more important in our daily lives. Water is certainly abundant, for it covers 70.8 per cent of the earth's surface to a depth of about 2½ miles. And, like air, it is truly one of life's necessities, for without water there would be no life. Water is many things to many people. It serves as a "thermostat" to temper world climates and it forms a vital part of the air that we breathe. Most of the world's commerce moves over water, and agriculture and industry must have water to survive. Because water reacts readily with other matter, chemists call it the "universal solvent."

The earth scientist recognizes the importance of water in yet another way. He sees water as the great "leveler"—the major force that has shaped Earth's face throughout geologic time. In the past, as today, streams have widened and deepened their channels by erosion and groundwater has passed through buried rock formations, dissolving minerals along the way. And over the ages the sea has relentlessly attacked the land, wearing away solid rock in one area only to deposit it as loose sediment somewhere else.

Great quantities of water, constantly on the move, are required if water is to do all the things it must. Thanks to the *hydrologic cycle*, we have a very efficient mechanism that fulfills this need. Most of Earth's water is of meteoric origin, that is, it has been derived from the atmosphere as rain or snow. Using energy provided by the sun, water is evaporated from the sea and condenses

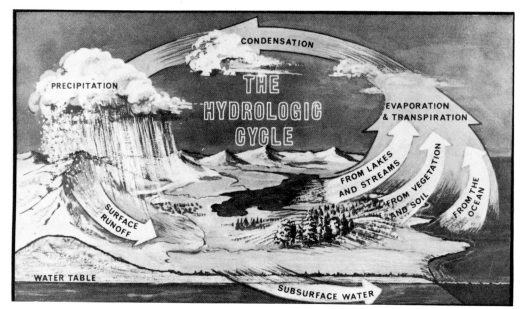

U. S. Geological Survey

The hydrologic, or water, cycle is the mechanism that keeps the waters of the earth in constant circulation.

in the atmosphere as clouds of water vapor. Winds (powered by solar energy) transport the water-laden clouds to the land. There the atmospheric water may be released by precipitation in the form of rain or snow.

Although much of the water falls back into the ocean, great amounts fall on the land. Most of this water is returned to the atmosphere by evaporation or *transpiration*, a process whereby plants breathe water vapor back into the air. The rest is channeled into streams or underground water-bearing strata where it may eventually return to the sea. The water cycle has neither beginning nor end and it has probably been in constant operation for more than four billion years. During this time, water has, in one way or another, served as the unifying thread that binds the various geologic agents together.

An estimated 22 to 30 per cent of the meteoric water is returned to the sea as *runoff*. Excessive runoff causing continued erosion can be very destructive to fertile farm lands. Luckily, most of this water is channeled into streams. This running water can be a highly effective geologic tool. Consider, for example, the Grand Canyon of the Colorado River in Arizona. Almost a mile deep, about nine miles wide, and 217 miles long, this magnificient gorge is largely the work of stream erosion. Streams wear away the land, picking up sediment and carrying it along as they flow. Eventually, however, the stream must deposit its load. This—the process of *deposition*—represents the constructional phase of the work of running water. It is not surprising, then, that running water has done more to sculpture the landscape than all other geologic agents combined.

Water that soaks into the ground can also bring about change. As it moves downward in response to gravity, groundwater may dissolve the rocks through which it flows. Consequently, areas which are underlain by soluble rocks like limestone may become

The Badlands of South Dakota have been developed as a result of erosion by running water with the help of atmospheric weathering.

William S. Keller, National Park Service

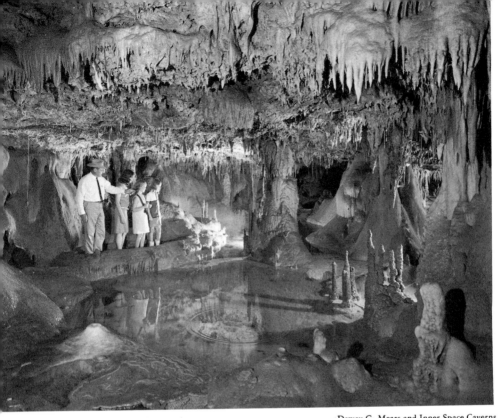

Although it does its work beneath the surface, groundwater is an active geologic agent in some areas. Inner Space Caverns in Texas has been dissolved from limestone and decorated with many unusual cave formations.

honeycombed with caverns. Yet some of the dissolved rock material is returned to the rocks as the mineral-laden groundwater deposits its load to form stalactites, stalagmites, and other cave formations. The work of underground water has provided us with such interesting features as Carlsbad Caverns, Mammoth Cave, and most of the world's great caverns. Much more important, some of the groundwater is funneled into water-transporting rock layers called *aquifers*. These porous and permeable formations serve as invaluable reservoirs for much of our supply of fresh water.

The never-ending battle of land and sea is almost as old as Earth itself. Anyone who has observed the ceaseless churning of the oceans can readily understand its power as a geologic tool. Most of the sea's work is done by means of waves and wave-produced currents which keep erosion-producing rock fragments in continual abrasive motion. Sooner or later the sea must deposit the load of sediments it has produced. This marine deposition is responsible for sand bars, beaches, and many of our lands.

In short, water—working in and on the earth's crust—is the master tool with which Nature has sculptured the landscape.

WORK OF THE WEATHER—SLOW BUT SURE

Weather is all around us and, unless it is particularly good or bad, we seldom give it much thought. But good, bad, or indifferent, and whether we notice it or not, weather as a geologic agent is on duty around the clock. Rock is weathered whenever and wherever atmospheric agents come in contact with solid earth material. Rocks are dissolved by rain water and melting snow, scratched by wind-blown sand, and pried apart by frost and ice. The changes that occur at the interface between the atmosphere and lithosphere normally work slowly—but surely—to alter the earth's surface.

The work of *weathering* can be seen the world around. It had a hand in the shaping of the Grand Canyon, has helped to round off the sharp peaks of the Alps, carved the totem pole-like landscape at Bryce Canyon National Park, and put the "bad" in the Badlands of South Dakota.

Some weather-produced changes are largely physical. Known as *disintegration,* this type of rock weathering simply reduces the original rock to increasingly smaller fragments. *Decomposition,* on the other hand, is a form of weathering whereby rock is decayed and altered by chemical change.

Not all rocks weather at the same rate. Climate, the nature of the rock, and the elevation of the land all have an effect on the weathering process. The rate of weathering has also varied

Jennie A. Matthews

These tombstones, in a New England burial ground, illustrate how one rock may weather more quickly than another. The inscription on the marker on the left was carved in slate and is still legible. Although erected much later, weathering has completely obliterated the inscription from the marker on the right which is composed of less resistant stone.

In desert regions the work of the wind can be an important geologic factor. These dunes in New Mexico consist of sand particles that were eroded from another area.

U. S. Department of Agriculture

throughout geologic time. Factors such as differences in the amount of protection provided by vegetation and changing climates have been especially important.

Disintegration and decomposition do wear away the land and this can cause problems. Weathering does, nevertheless, play a vital and beneficial role in certain biological and geological processes. Soil—the end result of rock weathering—more than compensates for the negative side of weathering. Soil is something of a "bridge" that connects the biosphere with the inorganic spheres of air, water, and land. Indeed, some scientists think there would be no life without soil and no soil without life—certainly not on the land.

THE WAYS OF GLACIERS

Many of the world's highest mountains are draped with massive blankets of ice. Known as glaciers, these moving ribbons of ice originate in snow fields at higher elevation. Here the annual snowfall and refreezing of melted snow are greater than the rate of over-all melting.

As snow and ice piles up, it gradually becomes deeper and more compact. Pressure exerted by the overlying snow pack eventually squeezes the lower layers together to form rounded pellets of ice. As more snow is added, the weight on the granular ice steadily increases until the lower part of the snow-ice pack becomes pressed together to form solid glacial ice. When sufficient glacier ice has accumulated, the ice—reacting to the effect of gravity—slowly starts to move downslope. At this point a glacier is born.

Most *valley* (or *alpine*) glaciers make their way downslope by following old stream-cut valleys. But rather than "run" like streams of water, these powerful rivers of ice slowly creep down the mountainside. Although the movement of the ice can vary greatly, glaciers typically travel only inches per day or week.

On steeper slopes, however, a valley glacier can move ten or even twenty feet per day. More rarely, sudden short-lived glacial surges have been known to move glaciers as much as 100 to 370 feet per day.

Glaciers greatly alter the rocks over which they pass. Rocks may become frozen into the ice and torn from the valley floor or wall. Additional rock debris may also fall on top of the glacier. Each rock picked up by the glacier may become embedded in the ice to become a sharp "tooth" that scratches and gouges the rocks over which it passes. As glaciation continues, the originally V-shaped stream-cut valley is scooped out to form the typical U-shaped glacial valley.

But like other geologic agents, glaciers cannot transport their load of rock fragments indefinitely. Most glacial deposition oc-

Yentna Glacier in Alaska is a classic example of a large alpine glacier with small tributary glaciers entering from either side. The dark streaks on the ice consist of rock debris that will later be deposited when the ice melts.

Yosemite Valley—major scenic attraction at Yosemite National Park—was first carved by streams and later reshaped by a great valley glacier. In this view from Inspiration Point, outstanding geologic features include El Capitan on the left, Half Dome in the distance, and Cathedral Rocks on the right above Bridalveil Fall.

curs when the ice melts, leaving piles of glacial sediments. Some of these sediments assume distinctive shapes which dot the landscape with telltale traces of past glaciation. California's Yosemite Valley, the Teton Range in Wyoming, and the Alps are classic examples of how glacial ice has left its mark on the land.

Continental glaciers, or *ice sheets*, are the giants of the world of ice. The largest of these, the Antarctic ice sheet, blankets most of the continent of Antarctica—an area almost twice the size of the United States. This ice mass is as much as 13,000 feet thick in some places. The ice sheet that covers Greenland has a surface area of about 670,000 square miles and an estimated maximum thickness of perhaps two miles. In some regions isolated mountain peaks project above the ice sheet causing land forms known as *nunataks*, an Eskimo word that literally means "island" in a "sea" of ice. Some nunataks, like Mount Erebus in the Transantarctic Mountains, consist of active volcanoes.

The glaciers of today are restricted to higher elevations on the continents and cover little more than 10 per cent of the earth's surface. But during the Ice Age, the most recent chapter in earth history, almost one-third of the present land surface of the earth was intermittently blanketed with ice. During these frigid times, valley glaciers dotted many of the continental mountains, the Antarctic and Greenland ice sheets were much thicker and widespread, and thick ice sheets spread across Eurasia and northern North America. As we shall see in a later chapter, the ice sheets and glacial climates of the Ice Age had a profound effect on the life of that time. The land changes that glaciers brought about also left their mark on the earth's surface, and some of these changes still affect us today.

Geologists studying the Antarctic ice sheet pause before a "rock island" called a nunatak.

U. S. Geological Survey

WHEN THE LAND SLIDES

Four battered palm trees, a white statue of Jesus Christ, and a sea of mud and rock are the lonely remains that mark the burial place of a city. The palm trees grew in the main plaza of Yungay, one of Peru's more beautiful resort cities. The statue of Christ marked Yungay's burial ground—and it still does. Towering above this desolate scene is 21,800-foot Mount Huascarán, the highest peak in Peru. The fresh raw scar on Huascarán's north peak is significant: it provided the 20 to 45 million cubic yards of ice and rock debris that buried Yungay and most of its 19,000 inhabitants.

The scarred face of Mount Huascarán and the tongue of mud and rock at its base are silent testimony to the work of another geologic agent—gravity. Fortunately, not all *mass movement* (as this gravity-induced process is called) is as destructive as the Peruvian avalanche. But landslides and avalanches are a common form of mass wasting and have caused great loss of life and much property damage in many parts of the world.

Mass wasting takes place as earth materials move downslope in response to gravity. Changes of this type are most likely to occur in areas with slopes that are steep enough to permit downward movement of rock debris.

What starts the downhill movement of such great quantities of rock and soil? Several factors, working alone or in combination, can trigger mass movement. Strong vibrations caused by earthquakes have touched off many of the world's more destructive mass movements. The great Peruvian earthquake that triggered the avalanche which entombed Yungay affected an area of 25,000 square miles, destroyed 186,000 buildings, and killed 50,000 people. It is not surprising, then, that this major earth convulsion caused a great disruption in the Huascarán ice field high above Yungay. Roaring down the mountainside at a speed of almost 250 miles per hour, the ice and snow gathered rocks

This statue of Christ, four palm trees, and parts of a burial crypt are all that remain of Yungay, Peru. The city was buried by a massive ice and rock avalanche triggered by the May 31, 1970, Peru earthquake.

and soil along the way. When it was all over more than 80 million cubic feet of water, mud, and rocks had been smeared over an area of about nine square miles.

Avalanches differ from landslides in that they contain large amounts of ice and snow. Landslides, on the other hand, are relatively rapid mass movements consisting primarily of rocks and soil. Mudflows and earthslides are another type of rapid mass wasting that can do much damage. In parts of California expensive houses have been carried away and destroyed by the unstable soil on which they were built. Other homes have been flooded with thick, syrupy sheets of mud that have flowed into the canyons where they are located. Excessive rainfall, the rather steep slope of the land, and the destruction of protective vegetation by drought and forest fires, have all made it easier for gravity to do its geologic work.

Much more common and far less destructive are slow mass movements. *Soil creep*, a gradual form of mass wasting, typically takes place on most slopes that are not steep enough to promote landslides. As the soil slowly moves downhill, it may deform rock strata, tilt trees, and displace fences. Soil creep is helped along by water, which adds weight to the soil and might serve as a lubricant to aid the soil and rocks as they gradually slip down the hillside.

Compared to the other geologic agents that have been mentioned, mass wasting plays a relatively small role in landscape development.

Solid earth, then, is not as immovable, unyielding, everlasting, and unchanging as some people would have us believe. Rock weathering, mountain-building, metamorphism, and countless other processes have constantly been at work throughout the billions-of-years-old history of the earth. Evidence of these changes have been recorded in the rocks of Earth's crust. It is the earth scientist's task to search for the clues that will enable him to piece together the history of our planet.

Although not as spectacular as an avalanche or landslide, relatively slow mass wasting can do extensive damage in certain areas.

Soil Conservation Service, U.S. Department of Agriculture

Chapter 13

EARTH WRITES
ITS OWN HISTORY

It was summertime in England. Near the quaint village of Lyme Regis in Dorsetshire, a little girl and her dog carefully picked their way along the shore of the English Channel. Occasionally she would pause to examine the rocks at the base of the famous White Cliffs that line the Channel. Then she would move on, her alert eyes continually scanning the rock-littered beach.

Was this youngster, like many summer visitors, looking for sea shells? Had she lost something? Or was she simply walking her dog? Mary Anning was not doing any of these things. She was looking for fossils—the remains of creatures that lived in ancient seas that covered England many millions of years ago. And Mary found fossils. On this particular day in 1811 she made a great discovery: the fossilized skeleton of a fishlike reptile that cruised the sea when dinosaurs ruled the land. This strange fossil was unlike anything known to man and its discovery created much excitement among scientists. Here were the stony remains of a beast which resembled a fish but definitely had certain lizard-like characteristics. This explains why it was later named *Ichthyosaurus*, a word which literally means "fish-lizard."

Like many fossil collectors, Mary Anning was not a scientist. Yet like certain other amateur "bone hunters," she did make some very important finds. In 1821 she uncovered the remains of another sea-going reptile known as a plesiosaur. And seven years later Mary found—for the first time in England—the skeleton of an extinct flying reptile called a pterosaur.

Mary's fossil finds are clues to an exciting chapter in the development of life on earth. These fossils, and others like them, are but one way that Earth has recorded its history in its rocky crust.

FOSSILS—CLUES TO THE PAST

How did Mary Anning's strange creatures come to be embedded in the chalk of the White Cliffs? And how can Earth "write" its own history? To answer these questions let us flip back the pages of time many millions of years to the "Age of Reptiles." During this exciting chapter in Earth's history the world's geography and inhabitants were quite different than they are today. In those days a great sea covered much of what is now dry land and along the shore many streams emptied into the ocean. As they flowed to the sea, these streams eroded the land and carried along small rock particles called sediment. Many of these rock fragments were deposited in the stream bed. Others

Extinct swimming reptiles such as this ichthyosaur were common in the sea during the "Age of Reptiles."

Courtesy of the American Museum of Natural History

were transported to the sea and settled out on the ocean floor.

Some of the plants and animals in this ancient sea extracted calcium carbonate from the water to build their limy shells. When they died this chalklike substance was added to the sediment on the ocean bottom. As time passed, the sediments continued to build up, until in some areas they were thousands of feet thick. The great weight of the overlying sediment pressed down on the lower layers of rock fragments, gradually squeezing them together. Meanwhile, chemicals in the water acted as cement to bind the sediment still more closely together. After a long period of time—perhaps hundreds of thousands of years— the rock-forming process was complete and the sediment had been compressed and cemented to form sedimentary rock.

Many animals, including *Ichthyosaurus* and the plesiosaur, lived in this prehistoric sea. Other organisms lived along the shore and some—Mary's flying reptile among them—flew over the sea and land. If these creatures died in the ocean their bodies sank to the sea floor and became mixed with the sand and mud. Although most of their remains were destroyed or decayed, some of their teeth, bones, or shell might have been preserved as fossils.

Perhaps you, like Mary Anning, have picked up a rock that resembled a bone or a shell. If you have, you may have wondered how it got into the rocks and whether it was a "real" bone or shell. This is a natural reaction, for there is evidence that man has puzzled over fossils for a very long time. Fossil shell and bones have been found with the remains of primitive and prehistoric men. It is possible that these ancient people believed that fossils possessed some type of supernatural power that would remove curses or ward off evil spirts.

In later times, fossils attracted the attention of certain Greek and Roman scholars. These wise men recognized the similarity between certain fossil shells and the shells of animals living at that time. Although not certain of their exact origin, these early

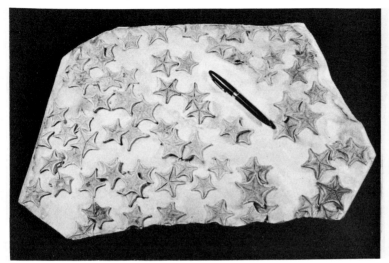

The fossil starfish in this piece of limestone were deposited in Texas during the Cretaceous Period.

thinkers at least suspected that the fossil shells represented the remains of ancient animals. In addition, when they found the fossil remains of sea-dwelling creatures in the mountains they correctly assumed that the land in that area had once been covered by the ocean.

However, most people of that long-ago time refused to believe this. They were a superstitious lot and firmly convinced that these out-of-place shells were freaks of nature created by mysterious "plastic forces." They saw the devil's hand in this evil scheme and thought that he had placed the fossils in the rocks to lead men astray!

As time passed and scientific thought progressed, the true nature of fossils began to be understood. Finally, in the late eighteenth and early nineteenth centuries fossils were generally recognized as relics of prehistoric life.

At this point you may wonder how a bone or shell could escape destruction for such an incredible span of time. *Fossiliza-*

The remains of many Ice Age creatures have been removed from the La Brea tar pits in Los Angeles. Above is a reconstruction of how the area might have appeared as the animals became trapped in the sticky asphalt.

tion can come about in a number of ways, but is more apt to occur if the plant or animal has hard body parts. But hard parts are not a "must," for under the proper conditions such delicate creatures as insects, worms, and jellyfish have been fossilized. Preservation is also more likely if the remains are buried soon after death.

However, fossilization also depends on the nature of the organism's hard parts and where and how it was buried. In some places, prehistoric remains have been found in deposits of tar and quicksand. These materials not only bury the remains, they also serve to trap the animals. Asphalt or tar is an especially effective preservative, for it also acts as an antiseptic to retard decomposition of the animal's hard parts. The Rancho La Brea tar pits of Los Angeles are famous for the many fossil bones that have been collected there. Fossils that have been recovered at La Brea include the bones of more than 500,000 animals that lived during the Ice Age. These include giant ground sloths, the great woolly mammoth, the saber-toothed "tiger," and many other extinct species. The remains of birds, reptiles, and plants have also been extracted from the sticky tar.

Occasionally the bodies of certain Ice Age animals have been preserved in ice or frozen soil. Needless to say, such fossils are relatively rare. However, they are especially valuable because the soft parts—which usually decay quickly—are commonly well preserved. Consequently there is some indication as to what the skin, hair, and other soft tissues might have been like when the animal was alive.

Assuming that the organic remains escape destruction and become buried in a suitable preserving material, there are a number of ways by which fossilization may take place. The rarest type of preservation is that in which the *original soft parts* of an organism are preserved. The woolly mammoths (extinct elephant-like animals) that have been found in the frozen soils of Siberia and Alaska are good examples of this type of preservation. The bodies of these shaggy beasts have been locked in the frozen tundra for as much as 25,000 years and when the icy earth

Ward's Natural Science Establishment

This fossil insect is preserved in amber, the hardened resin of a cone-bearing tree. It was found in an area that is generally too cold for such insects today.

thaws their great carcasses are exposed. Some specimens are so well preserved that their flesh has been eaten by dogs and their tusks sold for their ivory content.

Can you imagine a fossil gnat or mosquito? Or, perhaps a fossil spider web? Curiously enough, these fragile objects—many of them millions of years old—have been also fossilized. Some of these remains have been preserved in amber, a fossil resin that oozed from certain types of cone-bearing trees like the cedar or pine. In times past, insects frequently became trapped in the sticky resin. Over the years, the gumlike resin hardened, leaving the insect encased in a tomb of amber.

The dried out, mummified remains of certain extinct ground sloths have been discovered in caves and volcanic craters in New Mexico and Arizona. These unusual natural mummies are so well preserved that parts of the original skin, hair, tendons, and claws can be studied in considerable detail. As might be suspected, the preservation of original soft parts has resulted in some remarkable fossils. As noted earlier, however, this type of fossilization is actually quite rare.

The fossilization of an organism's *original hard parts* is much more common, because plants and animals usually contain some type of hard skeletal material. This may be the woody tissue of plants, the shell of a snail or clam, the bones of a fish, or the tooth of a reptile. Such hard parts may be composed of various materials which are capable of resisting destruction.

It is common, however, for organic remains to undergo great change after burial. Consequently, fossils consisting of the *altered hard parts* of organisms are especially numerous in the earth's crust. Some of these are *petrified*, or literally turned to stone. Fossils of this kind are formed when mineral-bearing ground waters seep into the open spaces in bone, shell, or wood. As time passes, the underground water deposits its mineral content in the empty spaces of the hard parts. This makes the original organic

This fish from Tertiary rocks in Wyoming has been fossilized by the process of carbonization.

matter heavier and usually more resistant to weathering. Fossils of this kind can be seen in the great stone trees at Petrified Forest National Park in Arizona.

Some hard parts, particularly those of plants, have been altered by *carbonization*. This process may take place as organic material gradually decays after burial. As decomposition occurs, the plant or animal matter slowly loses its gases and liquids, leaving a thin film of carbon in or on the rocks. Such naturally occurring impressions are somewhat like "carbon copies" of the original plant or animal. Carbonization is the same type of chemical and physical change that produces coal. And, because coal is formed largely of carbonized plant remains, fossil plants are commonly preserved in this way.

Not all fossils consist of the actual remains of once-living plants and animals. Some organisms have left only a trace or indirect evidence of their existence. Thus, tracks made by a dinosaur are just as much a fossil as a bone or tooth from one of these extinct reptiles. In some instances the dinosaur tracks may tell us the

Although the actual remains of the dinosaur are missing, this footprint is proof that the animal was once in the area where the print was found.

Jennie A. Matthews

shape and size of the animal's foot. Such tracks may also provide information about the dinosaur's weight and length.

Shells, leaves, and bones are commonly pressed down into the ocean bottom before the sediment is turned to rock. After the sediment hardens and the shell is dissolved, an impression of the shell remains in the rock. This imprint is known as a *mold*, and shows what the exterior of the shell originally looked like. If this mold should later become filled with more sediment or some type of mineral, a *cast* is produced. Molds and casts are abundant in many fossil-bearing rocks and are among the most common of fossils.

Coprolites (fossil dung or body waste) are rather unusual trace fossils. These ancient droppings can provide information as to the food habits of the animals that left them. The well-rounded, highly polished stones called *gastroliths* have been found associated with the remains of dinosaurs and other extinct reptiles. These "stomach stones" are believed to have been used in the stomachs of reptiles for grinding their food into smaller pieces. Thus, "circumstantial evidence" such as tracks, molds, and coprolities has also played an important role in reconstructing life of the past.

We know, of course, that fossils cannot talk. They do, nevertheless, tell us much about the earlier chapters in the history of the earth. How can these silent witnesses of the past reveal their secrets? Fossils not only represent the remains of once-living plants or animals, they also provide clues as to when, where, and how the organisms lived. The paleontologist uses these clues to learn more about the ancient organism and to solve other mysteries of geologic history.

In working with fossils, the paleontologist uses many of the techniques and principles of the biologist. He believes—and rightly so—that if we are to understand properly the many different kinds of prehistoric life, we must know something about the plants and animals that are living today. In short, we assume that the plants and animals of the past lived under conditions similar to those of their nearest living relatives or the living forms that they most closely resemble. It is known, for example, that the dinosaurs have been extinct for about 70 million years. Even so, a great deal is known about these ancient beasts. Their skeletons clearly indicate that they were reptiles. Consequently, it is believed that these extinct creatures had the same basic characteristics and assumed many of the same habits as the reptiles of today.

This idea is based on the Principle of Uniformitarianism which was proposed by James Hutton in 1795. This long word has a rather short definition. It simply means that "the present is the key to the past." Thus, a study of the nature and habits of the modern biosphere can lead to a better understanding of the plants and animals of long ago.

Most fossils are found in marine sedimentary rocks that

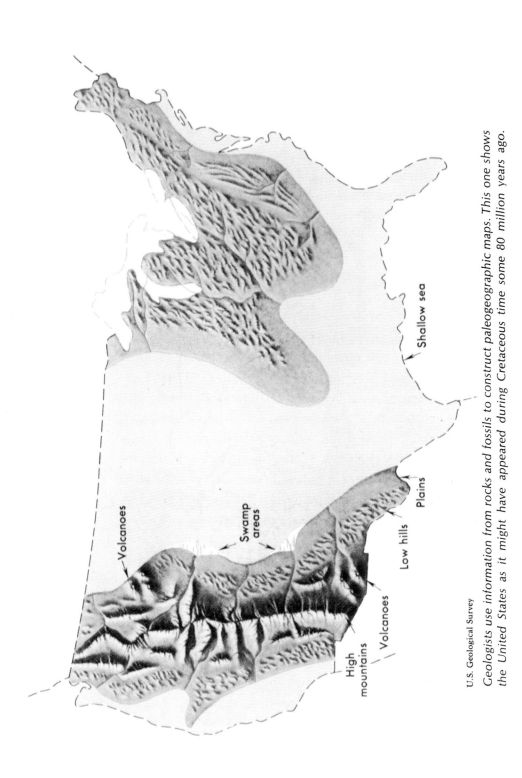

Geologists use information from rocks and fossils to construct paleogeographic maps. This one shows the United States as it might have appeared during Cretaceous time some 80 million years ago.

formed from sediment deposited in ancient seas. But the remains of land-dwelling organisms have also been preserved. Fossil trees, the bones of extinct elephants, and dinosaur tracks and trails occur in many parts of the world. Like marine fossils, these terrestrial fossils yield much information about the land-dwelling organisms from which they were formed. Equally important, they may reveal something about the environment in which the plant or animal lived. For example, the reef-building corals have apparently always lived as they do today. They prefer warm, shallow, rather clear, salt water and seem to have thrived in such an environment for hundreds of millions of years. Consequently, the presence of a fossil coral reef suggests that the rocks containing them were formed from sediments deposited in relatively shallow, warm, clear, salt water.

The fossil remains of corals and other marine organisms enable the historical geologist to map the location of prehistoric seas. On the other hand, terrestrial fossils can be helpful in finding the position of ancient landmasses. Information derived from such fossils is useful in preparing *paleogeographic maps*. These "ancient-geographic" maps show the geography of a region as it might have appeared during a specific time in geologic history.

Penguins in Africa and tropical plants in Antarctica? Not today to be sure, but things have not always been as we see them now. Although not native to these areas at present, fossil penguins and other cold-weather creatures have been found in areas that are much too warm for them today. Coal is formed from the accumulated remains of plants typical of warm, humid areas. Thus, the presence of coal in the polar regions suggests a much warmer climate in the geologic past. Fossils of this type provide important clues as to past climates of the areas in which they are found.

Fossils can also be used to determine the age of the rocks in which they occur. Because certain species lived only during a specific part of geologic history, they are characteristic of rocks formed during that particular time. Dinosaurs, for example, lived only during the Mesozoic Era (see Chapter 14). Thus, dinosaur remains are distinctive time indicators for rocks formed during that era. Although they lived but a relatively short time in geologic history, dinosaurs inhabited many parts of the world during their rather short life span. Fossils of this type are called *index* or *guide fossils* because they normally occur only in rocks of a particular age.

The study of fossils has played an especially valuable role in tracing the development of life on earth. Paleontologists have learned that only the most primitive plant and animal fossils occur in the most ancient rocks of the earth's crust. However, as one studies fossils from progressively younger rocks, the fossils indicate a gradual change to more complex and advanced forms of life. Fossils that occur in the most recently formed rocks, become increasingly similar to the plants and animals of today. These fossils, when placed in the proper time sequence, suggest that certain species of plants and animals have gradually changed, or evolved, into the more modern organisms of later time.

Some fossils are so very small that they can only be studied with a microscope. Known as *microfossils*, these tiny fossil remains are extensively used as guide fossils by petroleum geologists in their search for oil. Microfossils are usually so small that they are not destroyed by the drill bits used to drill oil wells. Thus, they may be returned to the surface in an undamaged condition. They are then placed under the microscope and studied as possible clues to the location of oil-bearing rocks.

Interestingly enough, the most important use of fossils was discovered quite by accident. This happened in 1799 when William Smith, a surveyor, was planning the route for a canal to be constructed in southern England. As he studied the rocks through which the canal would be dug, the observant young

Englishman was astonished to discover that many rock layers contained fossils that were characteristic of that particular layer. He noted also that certain fossils in one layer of rock differed from those above and below it. Smith soon learned that the more distinctive fossils could be used to identify the various rock formations along the canal route. He found, moreover, that these fossils could be used to predict the location and physical characteristics of the rocks in a particular area. In short, "Strata" Smith had developed the important geologic technique of *correlation*. The process of "matching" the rocks and fossils of one geologic formation with those of another, correlation has helped the geologist solve some of the timeless mysteries of the geologic past.

READING THE RECORD

To the earth historian, the rock layers in the earth's crust are the pages of time. Each rocky "page" provides some information about Earth's history, but these clues to the past are not always easy to find. The "book" of earth history is about 4½ billion years old. And like many old books, some of its pages are faded and worn. Others are completely missing. These missing pages in the geologic record cause gaps that make it even more difficult to reconstruct the history of our planet.

In some places, for example, earthquakes and mountain-building upheavals have caused the rocks to become broken and folded. Elsewhere, rock layers have been shuffled out of place or completely destroyed by great heat and pressure. More often, however, rock layers have been worn away by the geologic work of ice, wind, running water, and weathering. These erosion-produced gaps in the rock record are called *unconformities*. Unconformities may also be caused by the nondeposition of sediments in a certain area. Such breaks in the geologic record become more numerous and troublesome in the older rocks in the earth's crust. This is not surprising, for the more ancient rocks

Unconformities represent gaps in the geologic record. The arrow indicates the major unconformity between the very old Precambrian rocks of the Inner Gorge of the Grand Canyon and the younger Cambrian rocks above them.

Jennie A. Matthews

have had more time to undergo physical change or be stripped away by erosion.

As might be expected, these missing chapters in the history of the earth greatly complicate the task of the earth scientist. Indeed, they force him to become a geological detective who must patiently probe the crust for clues that will enable him to fill in the "blanks" in the history of the earth.

What types of clues are hidden in the crust and where does the geological detective find them? Sedimentary rocks are an especially good source of information—particularly if they contain fossils. But some sedimentary formations are barren of clues and shed little or no light on the geologic history of an area.

As noted earlier, bedding, or *stratification*, is the most common feature of sedimentary rocks. The well-defined layers or rock strata are formed as water, ice, and other geologic agents gradually deposit their load of sediment. The type of bedding in such rocks will often provide a clue as to how the layers were originally deposited. This is possible because each geologic agent deposits its sediment in a rather distinctive manner.

The texture, or size, shape, and arrangement of the sediments from which a sedimentary rock is formed may also tell something about how the rock originated. For example, sediments laid down by glaciers typically vary greatly in size—they range from tiny grains of sand to massive boulders as large as a house. Wind, on the other hand, can carry only the finest, lightest types of sediment. Consequently, wind-blown deposits are usually rather fine grained.

Perhaps you have seen little waves or ripples of sand developed on the surface of a sand dune, beach, or the bottom of a stream. Similar ripples can also be seen in certain sedimentary rocks. These ripple marks may be clues as to the conditions of deposition when the sediment was originally deposited. You have also probably seen cracks in dried mud in the bottom of a stream or gutter. When mud or some other fine-grained sediment dries, it commonly shrinks in such a way as to form a series of honeycomb-like cracks. When preserved in the rocks, mud cracks suggest that the sediment was subjected to alternate periods of drying and flooding.

Strange as it may seem, the imprints of prehistoric raindrops may also be recorded in the rocks. Although rare, such raindrop impressions do occur and yield information about the rocks in which they are found.

The color of sedimentary rocks may also shed some light on the way in which the rocks were formed. In addition, color provides an indication as to some of the changes that the rock may have undergone. The color of a rock is determined largely by the minerals that it contains. Rocks which contain hematite (an iron mineral) will commonly be pink or red. Limonite, another iron-bearing mineral, typically produces rusty-colored to yellowish-

These ripple marks were probably formed on an ancient beach many millions of years ago. They now occur thousands of feet above sea level and hundreds of miles from the nearest ocean.

Jennie A. Matthews

brown rocks. Rocks high in organic matter, such as coal, are typically gray to black in color. But color is not always a reliable clue. Exposure to the atmosphere will cause rocks to become weathered, and weathering may affect the color of rocks when the minerals in them undergo chemical change.

Despite the missing pages in the record and the lack of certain clues, the geological detective has done much to solve many of Earth's more perplexing mysteries. But many of the earth's secrets are still tightly locked in its rocky crust, and earth scientists continue to probe for answers to these unsolved problems.

Chapter 14

HOW OLD IS OLD?

"What time it it?" "How old are you?" "What day does Christmas fall on this year?" These questions—and countless more like them—show how closely our lives are regulated by clock and calendar. It is not surprising, then, that we are are all interested in time.

Along with time goes age, and most of us are fascinated with objects that are extremely old. Old coins and stamps, antique furniture and automobiles, mummies and dinosaurs are but a few of the relics that have been collected or studied because of their great age. Time and age are of importance to all of us, but they have a very special meaning for the earth scientist. He is not only interested in time as it relates to the present, he is literally concerned with the very beginnings of time. His concept of age is equally unique, for geologists usually speak in terms of millions— even billions—of years. This is as it should be, because the geologist works with rocks, minerals, and fossils which are typically extremely ancient.

Some historians trace the development of a nation through a period of several hundred years. An archaeologist may go back several thousand years to establish the beginning of a certain ancient culture. But to reconstruct the earliest events in Earth's ancient history, the geologist must turn back the clock to the earliest known events on this 4½-billion-year-old planet.

We commonly mark the passing of time by relating it to a

series of events. Such events might be a particularly hot summer, or perhaps a great disaster such as a hurricane or earthquake. The geologist uses this same system to determine the *relative age* of geologic events. It permits him to assume that one geologic happening—say a volcanic eruption—occurred before or after another incident such as an earthquake.

To do this the earth historian must study and compare the relative positions of the rocks as they occur in the earth's crust. He must also determine what fossils—if any—are present. These can be especially helpful because they commonly provide clues as to the age of the rocks.

Relative dating is useful in that we can compare the age of one rock unit or geologic event to another. However, it does not give us an age in years. Rather, it is somewhat like knowing that the Civil War was fought before World War II. Although no *absolute time* (time measured in years) is given, it does place these incidents in their proper sequence in the history of our country.

MEASURING GEOLOGIC TIME

From the sun dial of the ancient Egyptians, through the great stone calendar of the Aztecs, all the way to the superaccurate cesium clock of the "Atomic Age," man has tried to measure the passage of time. Geologists have also devised methods to mark the passing of time and their efforts have given rise to the science of *geochronology*.

Although relative dating is useful, early geologists soon found that it would be helpful to know the approximate number of years that separated one geologic event from another. This prompted a number of early scientists to devise some means of approximating the age of the earth. One of the earliest attempts to assign an absolute age to the earth was made by Edmund Halley in 1715. This famous English astronomer correctly assumed that the oceans began as a body of fresh water. He also recognized that their salinity (or salt content) had steadily increased as salts were eroded from the land and transported to the sea by streams. This led Halley to propose that the salinity of the oceans might be a clue to their age. If so, this should give some indication as to the age of the earth. Unfortunately, Halley did not have sufficient information to use his so-called "salinity method" to compute the age of the seas.

But in 1898, John Joly believed that he had gathered sufficient data to make a reasonable estimate of the age of the oceans. This Irish scientist calculated that it had taken 80 to 90 million years for the sea to reach its present degree of salinity. Thus, the earth was bound to be somewhat older than that.

Other scientists attempted to learn how long it had taken to deposit all of the rock layers in the earth. Their estimates were based on the amount of time required for certain sediments to be deposited. How long, for example, had it taken to deposit the amount of sediment needed to form 100 feet of sandstone? When rates of sedimentation had been established, an attempt was then made to find out the total thickness of rock layers that had formed since deposition began. Next, these thicknesses were added together and multiplied by the rate at which the layers were supposed to have accumulated. Needless to say, there were many uncertainties involved in such a method, for there is no way to obtain complete and valid information of this type. But despite its shortcomings, the "sedimentation method" did provide age estimates that ranged from slightly less than 100 million to more than 400 million years old. Although these methods were improvements over certain earlier dating techniques, they were still rather unreliable.

Modern geochronologists obtain the ages of rocks and minerals by *radiometric dating*. This technique is made possible because certain minerals in the earth's crust contain radioactive elements,

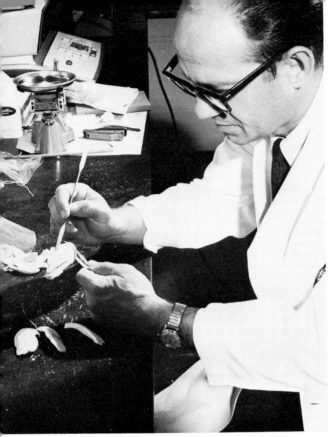

Geochronologist prepares a sample of fossil clam shell for radiometric dating.

such as uranium or thorium. These radioactive materials undergo spontaneous disintegration at a constant rate. Equally important, the rate at which they decay is not affected by changes in temperature, pressure, or other physical conditions. As certain radioactive minerals break down, helium is given off and a new series of elements is produced. Radioactive lead is the last element formed in this series. Geochronologists calculate the ratio between the radioactive lead and the amount of uranium that is left in a given sample. This ratio can be used to ascertain the age of the radioactive mineral. This technique is limited, of course, to those rocks that contain radioactive minerals. Similar radiometric dating methods are based on the rates at which potassium breaks down to argon, and the decay of rubidium to strontium. The oldest rocks dated by radiometric methods suggest that Earth

Although highly specialized equipment is needed, the Carbon-14 method is a valuable means of obtaining the geologic age of certain materials.

is more than three and one-half billion years old. Granites in South Africa have been dated at about 3 billion 200 million years and certain metamorphic rocks in southwestern Minnesota have yielded ages of 3 billion 600 million years.

Objects of less than 50,000 years old are commonly dated by the Carbon-14 method. This technique is based on the assumption that all living plants and animals contain a constant amount of Carbon-14—a radioactive *isotope*. (Isotopes are atoms of the same atomic number but of different atomic weights.) When an organism dies, Carbon-14, also called radiocarbon, slowly decays and is lost at a constant and known rate. This rate of decay is such that one-half of the original Carbon-14 has decayed at the end of 5730 years. Thus, Carbon-14 is said to have a *half-life* of 5730 years. In other words, if a sample of wood contained only one-half the amount of Carbon-14 found in living plants, the ancient wood should be 5730 years of age. Radiocarbon dating has been particularly useful in determining the age of archaeological specimens like the Dead Sea scrolls which were found in Israel. Carbon-14 dates obtained from the linen in the famous scrolls suggests that they are approximately 1983 years old.

Not all rocks lend themselves to radiometric dating and problems still exist with many of those that do. Be that as it may, the radioactive techniques have been invaluable in geochronological studies, for they have made it possible to calibrate the Geologic Time Scale into more absolute terms. This, in turn, enables the geologist to place certain geologic events in their proper position in earth history.

THE "CALENDAR" IN THE ROCKS

Most of us have had the frustrating experience of trying to tell someone about a past event but could not recall the precise day or month when the incident occurred. Early geologists faced this same problem when they began to describe and discuss the various episodes in the history of the earth. Like scholars who deal with the story of civilization, students of earth history soon learned that they must have some method of relating the various events of geologic time to each other.

The need to subdivide geologic history into a sequence of manageable chapters led to the development of the Geologic Time Scale. This rock "calendar" consists of named units of time during which the various rock units were formed. The geologist uses these time units to date events that took place in the geologic past.

The largest time unit is an *era*. The eras are divided into *periods* and these may be further subdivided into smaller time units called *epochs*. When arranged in their proper time sequence, these time units provide a standard by which the age of the rocks can be discussed.

The geologic time units of the "rock calendar" are not like the days and months on the calendar on your wall. The units of geologic time are arbitrary divisions of unequal duration, for there is no way of knowing precisely how much time was involved in each era, period, or epoch. The Geologic Time Scale does, nevertheless, permit earth scientists to tie a "time tag" on the various episodes of Earth's history. We can say, for example, that a certain rock is of Cretaceous age. This means that the rock was formed during the Cretaceous Period some 65 million years ago.

Each of the five eras of geologic time has been given a name that describes the degree of life development that characterizes the era. Thus, Paleozoic, which literally means "ancient life" refers to the relatively simple and ancient stage of life development during this era.

The eras, a guide to their pronounciation, and the literal translation of each name is as follows:

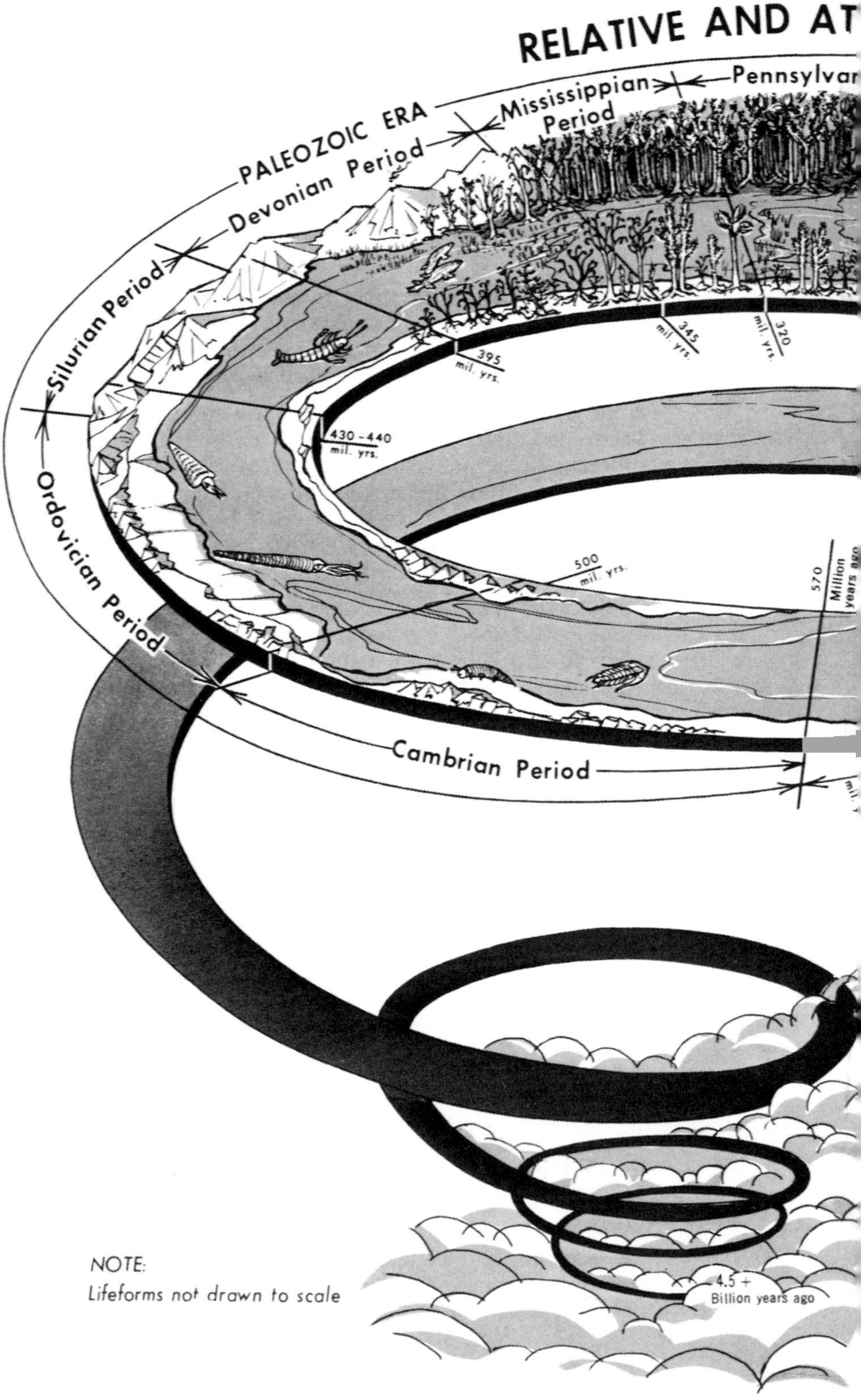
RELATIVE AND AT
PALEOZOIC ERA
Mississippian Period
Pennsylvar
Devonian Period
Silurian Period
Ordovician Period
Cambrian Period
395 mil. yrs.
345 mil. yrs.
320 mil. yrs.
430 - 440 mil. yrs.
500 mil. yrs.
570 Million years ago
4.5 + Billion years ago

NOTE:
Lifeforms not drawn to scale

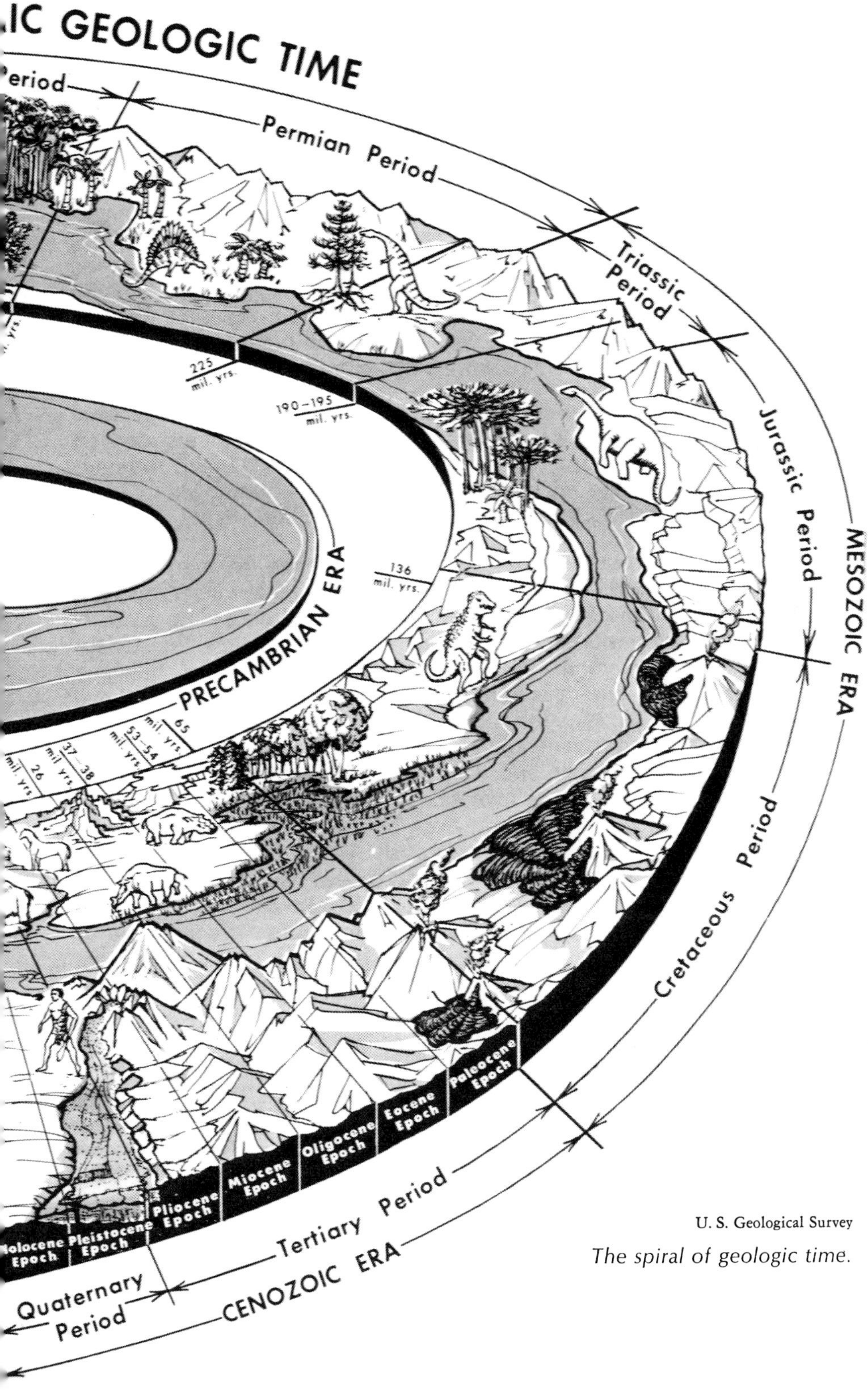
IC GEOLOGIC TIME
Period
Permian Period
Triassic Period
Jurassic Period
MESOZOIC ERA
Cretaceous Period
225 mil. yrs.
190–195 mil. yrs.
136 mil. yrs.
PRECAMBRIAN ERA
65 mil. yrs.
53–54 mil. yrs.
37–38 mil. yrs.
26 mil. yrs.
Holocene Epoch
Pleistocene Epoch
Pliocene Epoch
Miocene Epoch
Oligocene Epoch
Eocene Epoch
Paleocene Epoch
Quaternary Period
Tertiary Period
CENOZOIC ERA

U. S. Geological Survey

The spiral of geologic time.

Cenozoic (see'-no-zo-ic)—"recent-life"
Mesozoic (mes'-o-zo-ic)—"middle-life"
Paleozoic (pay'-lee-o-zo-ic)—"ancient-life"
Proterozoic (pro'-ter-o-zo-ic)—"fore-life"
Archeozoic (ar'-kee-o-zo-ic)—"beginning-life"

Archeozoic and Proterozoic rocks are commonly grouped together and referred to as Precambrian in age. The Precambrian rocks have been greatly deformed and are very old; hence, the record of this portion of earth history is quite difficult to interpret. Precambrian time represents that portion of geologic time from the beginning of earth history until the deposition of the earliest fossiliferous Cambrian rocks. If the earth is as old as is believed, Precambrian time may represent as much as 85 per cent of all geologic time.

As noted earlier, each era has been divided into periods, and most of the periods are named after the regions in which the rocks of each were first studied. For example, the Pennsylvanian rocks of North America were first studied in the state of Pennsylvania.

The Paleozoic Era has been divided into seven periods of geologic time. With the oldest at the bottom of the list, these periods and the source of their names are:

Permian (pur'-me-un)—from the Province of Perm in
   Russia
Pennsylvanian (pen-sil-vain'-yun)—from the state of
   Pennsylvania
Mississippian (miss-i-sip'-i-un)—from the Upper Mississippi Valley
Devonian (de-vo'-ni-un)—from Devonshire, England
Silurian (si-loo'-ri-un)—for the Silures, an ancient tribe
   of Britain

Ordovician (or-doe-vish'-un)—for the Ordovices, an ancient tribe of Britain

Cambrian (kam'bri-un)—from the Latin word *Cambria*, meaning Wales

The periods of the Mesozoic Era and the source of their names are:

Cretaceous (cre-tay'-shus)—from the Latin word *creta*, meaning chalky

Jurassic (joo-ras'-ik)—from the Jura Mountains between France and Switzerland

Triassic (try-ass'-ik)—from the Latin word *trias*, meaning three

The Cenozoic periods get their names from an old outdated system of classification which divided all of the earth's rocks into four groups. The two divisions listed below are the only names of this system which are still in use:

Quaternary (kwah-tur'-nuh-ri)—meaning fourth derivation

Tertiary (tur'-shi-ri)—meaning third derivation

Although the units discussed here are the major divisions of geologic time, geologists usually work with smaller units of rocks called *formations*. A geologic formation is identified and established on the basis of definite physical and chemical characteristics of the rocks. These formations are typically given geographic names which are combined with the type of rock that makes up most of the formation. For example, the Beaumont Clay was named from clay deposits that are found in and around Beaumont, Texas.

Chapter 15

TURNING BACK
THE PAGES OF TIME

We are living in a world of rapid change. Many of these changes such as advances in medicine and the invention of labor-saving devices have done much to improve our way of life. Others have led to serious problems such as overpopulation and the pollution of our land, water, and air.

The rather sudden increase in environmental problems has triggered a rush of speculations on the future of the earth. Where is life headed and what will Earth be like in, say, the year 2000? The earth scientist is particularly interested in the future of the earth, for it is his home, laboratory, and classroom. Yet he is not only concerned about our planet's future, he is equally interested in its past. More specifically, he is interested in the changes that have taken place in the geography, climate, and inhabitants of the earth. Although many of these changes began billions of years ago, they are responsible for much of what we see about us today.

THE STORY BEGINS

We need only to glance at the beginning of a United States history book to learn that our nation has changed greatly since the eventful year of 1776. And so it is with the earth, for the earliest chapters of earth history are written in the oldest rocks.

These billions-of-years-old rocks reveal that the earth and its inhabitants have changed greatly during this vast span of time. Luckily, the rocks and the fossils they contain have recorded these changes for us.

Earth's rocky "history book" reveals many interesting events. It indicates that the world's climate and geography have not always been as they are today. Indeed, they appear to have differed greatly from one major period of time to the next. There is also evidence to suggest that these physical changes in the environment had a profound effect on the plants and animals of the day. Little by little and bit by bit, earth historians have pieced the puzzle together. Although the picture is still far from complete, we do have a fairly accurate idea as to conditions on Earth throughout most of its long history. Let us now turn back the pages of geologic time to the very beginnings and follow some of the more important changes that it has undergone.

If you will look at the Geologic Time Scale on page 156, you will note that the oldest units of earth history appear at the bottom of our "geological calendar." These incredibly ancient rocks represent Precambrian time—that part of earth history from the beginning of geologic history until the formation of the earliest fossil-bearing rocks of the Cambrian Period.

Earth's story begins, then, with the events recorded in rocks formed during the *Archeozoic Era*. These rocks—some of which are at least three billion years old—consist of rocks that were originally igneous or sedimentary, but that have since been greatly altered by heat and pressure. In places these metamorphic rocks have been invaded by great plugs of granite. These intrusive rocks provide evidence of underground movements of molten rock. Unfortunately, the igneous activity, metamorphic changes, and structural deformation have greatly altered the original Archeozoic rocks. Consequently, little can be learned about their original characteristcs or any evidence of life that might have

More than a billion years old, this is the remains of a fossil algae that lived in Montana during Precambrian time.

Jennie A. Matthews

been present. However, some of the rocks do contain concentrations of carbon. These may have been formed from the remains of some as yet unknown type of Archeozoic plant or animal.

The story of Late Precambrian time is revealed in the Proterozoic rocks. Composed of igneous, sedimentary, and metamorphic formations, these rocks tell of a time of volcanic activity, glaciation, and considerable deposition of marine sediments. There is also evidence of an episode of mountain-building.

The first direct evidence of prehistoric life is found in rocks of Proterozoic age. These fossils consist largely of the carbon impressions of soft-bodied animals. Huge masses of organic limestone formed by sea-dwelling, lime-secreting algae are also known. In some parts of the world, the limy remains of these plantlike organisms form thick beds of limestone that are now found many thousands of feet above sea level.

THE PALEOZOIC—A TIME OF ANCIENT LIFE

The word "Paleozoic" literally means "ancient-life." This is an appropriate name for this portion of geologic history, for the life of this time was in an early stage of development. Fortunately, the Paleozoic rocks have been subjected to less erosion and deformation than the Precambrian rocks and there are many sedimentary strata which contain well-preserved fossils. Consequently, much more is known about the Paleozoic record than is known about Precambrian time.

More than 600 million years have passed since the *Paleozoic Era* began and this great span of time has been separated into seven periods of unequal duration. How do we know when one period stopped and another began? We cannot always tell for sure, but most periods appear to have been separated from each other by relatively short, naturally occurring periods of broad continental uplift. As the continents were raised the sea drained from the land. Each uplift was usually followed by a period of submergence when the ocean again rolled over parts of the landmasses. Sediments were deposited with each advance of the sea and these were later converted into sedimentary rock. There was much life in these prehistoric seas, and many of these organisms have been preserved as fossils. Some of them can be used to determine the age of the rocks that contain them.

Paleozoic time started with the *Cambrian Period* that began about 600 million years ago. This was a milestone in geologic history, for from Cambrian time on, we have a fairly good record of the development of life on earth. Cambrian rocks were first studied and described in Wales, and the name of the period is derived from the Latin word *Cambria*, which means Wales.

Although there is no way of knowing for sure, the Cambrian Period apparently lasted for about 100 million years. During this time some 30 per cent of North America was covered by an ancient sea that washed over the land. Sediments deposited in the

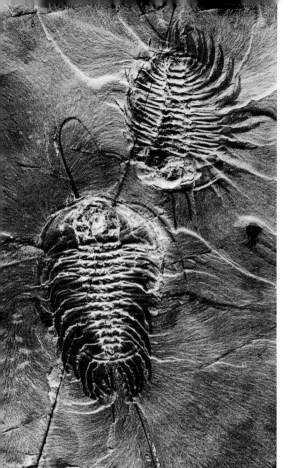

Smithsonian Institution

The trilobites—which became extinct at the end of Paleozoic time—were very abundant during the Cambrian Period.

Life of a sea floor during Ordovician time. This reconstruction, representing an area that is now near Chicago, shows a large, straight-shelled cephalopod eating a trilobite. Horn corals, sea lilies, and other invertebrates can also be seen.

Smithsonian Institution

Cambrian seas were later transformed into limestones, shales, sandstones, and other sedimentary rocks.

Cambrian fossils suggest that the life of this time was dominated by a great variety of invertebrates, or animals without backbones. The *trilobites*, relatives of the living horseshoe crab, and the shellfish known as *brachiopods* were especially abundant. Many other invertebrates and primitive plants inhabited Cambrian seas, but there is no evidence of any creatures with backbones. Nor is there anything to suggest that life had yet invaded the land.

The *Ordovician Period* was also first studied in Wales and derives its name from an old Celtic tribe, the Ordovices. Warm, shallow seas covered as much as 70 per cent of North America during the 75 million years of Ordovician time and their waters contained many species of plants and animals. Their fossil remains tell us that trilobites and brachiopods were still very abundant. But they were joined by many unusual species of corals, clams, snails, and *cephalopods*. The latter were extinct relatives of our modern squid and octopus. Some of these ancient cephalopods had straight, cone-shaped shells as much as fifteen feet long.

Perhaps the most important event of Ordovician time was the appearance of the first animal with a backbone—small armored fishes caller *ostracoderms*. These jawless fish are known from tiny fragments of bony plates and scales found in the Rocky Mountain region of the United States.

The nature of the Ordovician fossils and sedimentary rocks suggests that the climate of this period was uniformly temperate. Geologic evidence also indicates that there were no well-defined climatic zones as we know them today.

The *Silurian Period*, like the Ordovician, was named after an ancient Celtic tribe (the Silures) and the rocks were also first studied in Wales. The central part of the United States was

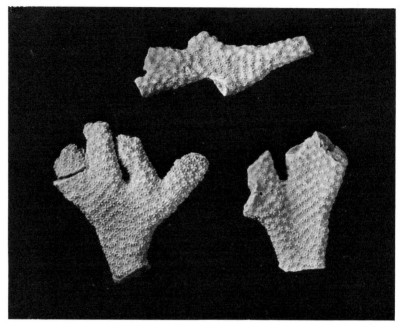

Bryozoans, or "sea mats" were especially numerous during the Ordovician Period.

flooded by a rather widespread sea during much of Silurian time, but near the end of the period, the water began to drain off the land. In places, landlocked bodies of water remained on the continent and slowly evaporated. As the water evaporated, thick concentrations of salt gypsum were deposited on the ocean floor in what is now Ohio, New York, Michigan, Pennsylvania, and Ontario in Canada.

The warm Silurian sea was teeming with brachiopods, corals, clams, and snails. Trilobites were still abundant but had reached their peak and were beginning to dwindle in numbers. The *eurypterids*, extinct scorpion-like creatures, are especially characteristic of Silurian time, and may have been the forerunners of the air-breathing animals. There were still no backboned creatures on the land but there were many fishes in the sea.

At some point during the Silurian Period life established its first foothold on the land. The way for terrestrial life was paved by rather simple, rootless plants whose remains have been found in England and Australia.

Silurian rocks and fossils suggest that the climate of this period must have been rather warm and mild. The salt and gypsum deposits of Late Silurian time hint of an episode of desert-like conditions for part of the country.

Named from exposures of rocks first studied near Devonshire,

The shaded areas show the extent of the Paleozoic seas during the Devonian Period.

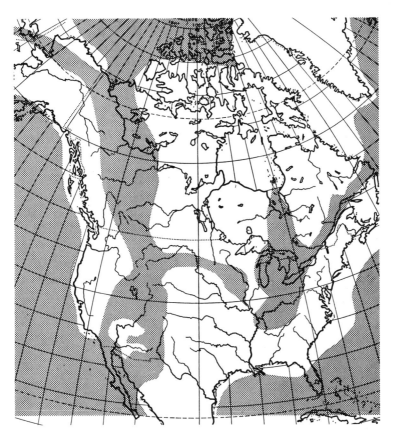

England, the *Devonian Period* was a time of great change. During the early part of the period, much of the North American continent was exposed. However, there was a rather widespread invasion of the sea in Middle Devonian time.

Devonian life was characterized by extensive expansion of the land plants. Ferns and seed plants were numerous and their remains are commonly found as fossils.

Brachiopods were the dominant Devonian invertebrates, but trilobites, corals, snails, and clams were also well represented.

Fishes underwent considerable expansion and their many fossils have caused some geologists to call the Devonian the "Age of Fishes." Especially notable were the great *arthrodires*. Some of these sharklike animals were as much as thirty feet long.

An important event of Devonian time was the appearance of the first four-footed vertebrate animal. This early amphibian

Sometimes mistakenly called fossil "butterflies," these brachiopods lived in Paleozoic seas that once covered New York state.

Smithsonian Institution

*Reconstruction of part of a sea floor in western New York at the begin-
ning of Middle Devonian time.*

lived in water and on the land, much as our toads and frogs of
today.

As far as is known, Devonian climates were mild and temperate throughout most of the period. The nature of some
Devonian fossils also suggests that some parts of the world were
warm and humid.

The *Mississippian Period* is named for exposures of rock first
studied in the Upper Mississippi River Valley of the United
States. Much of this part of the United States was covered by
an ancient Mississippian sea and the land was relatively near sea
level and had little relief. Thick vegetation grew in these warm,
moist swamplands and deposits of coal were formed from their
remains.

Life was thriving on land and in the sea during Mississippian
time and ferns, rushes, and other water-loving plants grew in

great profusion in the swamps. Insects were also present in great numbers and amphibians were rapidly expanding. Brachiopods and cephalopods were numerous in the sea, as were the *crinoids*, or "sea lilies."

Rocks of the *Pennsylvanian Period* were first studied in the state of Pennsylvania. This part of the United States was a region of low elevation during Pennsylvanian time and numerous swamps dotted the landscape. Vegetation grew profusely in these moist lowlands and their decaying remains were later transformed into valuable deposits of coal.

Marine life was plentiful in the warm Pennsylvanian seas. Spiny brachiopods, sea lilies, corals, snails, and clams were particularly numerous. The damp, jungle-like "coal forests" were swarming with such great hordes of insects that the Pennsylvanian is sometimes called the "Age of Insects."

The vertebrates were also thriving and the amphibians were especially well adapted to the swampy lowlands and were present in great numbers. A highlight of Pennsylvanian time is the appearance of the first reptile. Unlike amphibians, which must undergo a water larval stage, reptiles can spend their entire life on the land. The development of the early reptiles paved the way for the widespread reptilian evolution that occurred during Permian time.

Pennsylvanian climates were warm and moist. These conditions were ideal for the spread of the great "coal forests" and the many plants and animals that lived in them.

The *Permian Period* was the closing chapter of the Paleozoic Era. Many changes took place near the end of this period and animals that had been abundant for millions of years disappeared from the face of the earth. It is not surprising, then, that the Permian has been called "a time of great dying."

The Permian is named from the Province of Perm in Russia, and lasted for about 50 million years. During this time the seas

A fossil fern that is typical of plants that flourished during the "Coal Age" of Pennsylvanian time.

Field Museum of Natural History

were rather restricted. Rock-forming sediments were not widely deposited and exposures of Permian rocks are not common in eastern North America. However, there are extensive Permian formations in southeastern New Mexico, western Texas, Nebraska, Kansas, and the western United States. Many of the rock formations of such scenic areas as Carlsbad Caverns National Park and White Sands National Monument in New Mexico, Arizona's Grand Canyon, and the Garden of the Gods in Colorado are Permian in age.

Drastic changes in climate and geography took place near the end of Permian time. These changes had a profound effect on the plants and animals of that time and hastened the extinction of many species. Trilobites, which had been so numerous during much of Paleozoic time, disappeared from the earth, never to return again. And the brachiopods—especially the spiny and more unusual species—were drastically reduced in numbers and variety.

The places vacated by these vanishing creatures were quickly

Skeleton of Edaphosaurus, *a "sail-lizard" of Permian time.*

occupied by other species. Cephalopods, clams, snails, and reef-building corals underwent remarkable growth and new and unusual species were introduced.

Life also advanced on the land. Reptiles and amphibians continued to evolve and have left some interesting fossils. "Finback" reptiles such as *Edaphosaurus* and *Dimetrodon* sported large fin-like "sails" on their backs. Their remains are characteristic of a number of Permian formations.

The water-loving, swamp-dwelling plants so abundant during Pennsylvanian time were greatly reduced during the Permian. Their place was taken by *conifers* (cone-bearing plants) and other more modern species.

This "time of great dying" was also a period marked by extreme climatic changes. Times of desert-like dryness and glacial cold alternated with almost tropical, warm, and humid climates. The rock record suggests that there may have been swamplike conditions in Asia and Australia, and deserts in the southwestern

United States. Meanwhile, sheets of glacial ice blanketed parts of Australia, South Africa, and South America. Small wonder that certain Permian species were unable to adapt to such drastic changes in the environment.

The geographic changes of the Permian were almost as dramatic as those of the climate and life. Near the end of the period the final movements of the great Appalachian Revolution gave rise to the Appalachian Mountains. This great range stretches from Nova Scotia southward into Alabama. The rocks which were folded upward in this great *orogeny* were formed from sediment deposited in a branch of the sea that once occupied what is now the Appalachian region.

WHEN REPTILES RULED THE WORLD

The so-called "middle" era of the geologic calendar was a turning point in the history of life. Known literally as the time of "middle-life," the *Mesozoic Era* marked the transition from the relatively simple organisms of Paleozoic time to the more modern species of the Cenozoic Era.

Mesozoic seas were filled with countless species of plants and animals and land-dwelling organisms were equally abundant. But the true "stars" of this act in the drama of life were the reptiles. It is not surprising that this era is called the "Age of Reptiles," for dinosaurs ruled the land and equally strange reptiles filled the sea and air.

The "Age of Reptiles" began with the *Triassic Period* about 230 million years ago. Named from the Latin word *trias* (meaning three) it is called this because of the three-fold division displayed by the Triassic rocks in central Germany.

The Triassic deposits of the western United States have produced some spectacular scenery. The Grand Canyon, Painted Desert, and Petrified Forest in Arizona, as well as Utah's Zion

Relatives of the squids and octopuses, the extinct ammonites were numerous in seas of Mesozoic itme.

Jennie A. Matthews

Canyon all contain colorful formations of Triassic age.

The life of Triassic time was considerably advanced over the plants and animals of the Paleozoic. New species appeared in the sea and on land. In addition, some of the existing forms underwent considerable expansion. The predominant land plants were the conifers (cone-bearing trees), ferns, and the palmlike plants called *cycads*. Fossil conifers of Triassic age occur among the great stone trees at Petrified Forest National Park in Arizona.

Marine invertebrates filled the sea, and corals, clams, oysters, snails, and cephalopods were especially common.

Sea-dwelling vertebrates included many species of sharks and the bony fish were also well represented. Living in the sea were strange sea-going reptiles such as the ichthyosaur, a streamlined creature that resembled a swordfish. The equally peculiar plesiosaurs were also present and some of these grew to be forty feet in length. You will recall that it was two such reptiles that Mary Anning discovered in England during the early nineteenth century.

Reptiles also dominated life on the land. The bones of phytosaurs, a group of reptiles that superficially resemble crocodiles, are especially characteristic of certain Triassic formations. The first dinosaurs also appeared during the Triassic. They were relatively small, however, when compared to the gigantic species which dominated life of the Jurassic and Cretaceous Periods.

The great abundance of fossil reptiles and amphibians suggests warm mild climates for much of the earth during Triassic time. However, thick deposits of gypsum and salt indicate that desert-like conditions must have been present in certain parts of the world during this period.

Named from exposures in the Jura Mountains located between Switzerland and France, the *Jurassic Period* is well known for the large numbers of unusual reptiles that have been found in its sedimentary formations.

Although there were abundant and varied species of Jurassic plants, cycads were especially abundant. Tree ferns were present, as were ginkgos, conifers, scouring rushes, and ferns.

Many invertebrates filled the seas, and clams, snails, oysters, and cephalopods were especially common. Marine vertebrates were well represented by sharks, fishes, and turtles. Meanwhile, ichthyosaurs and plesiosaurs continued to thrive as they had during the Triassic.

But it was again the reptiles—especially the dinosaurs—that dominated Jurassic life. Some, like *Brontosaurus*, were four-footed plant-eaters that grew to be eighty feet long and weighed tens of tons. These creatures provided food for the ferocious meat-eaters like *Allosaurus*. This great beast of prey was about thirty-five feet long and his powerful jaws were well equipped

This scene, typical of the "Age of Reptiles," shows the plate-backed Stegosaurus in the foreground being stalked by Allosaurus, a two-legged meat eater. Three duck-billed dinosaurs can be seen in the left background, while Brontosaurus seeks safety in the water.

with sharp teeth. The peculiar plate-backed dinosaur, *Stegosaurus*, was another distinctive Jurassic reptile.

The earliest known pterosaurs, or flying reptiles, also appeared during the Jurassic time. These remarkable winged "dragons" had batlike wings supported by arms, and long thin "fingers." *Rhamphorhyncus*, with a wingspread of about two feet, is a typical Jurassic species.

Two very significant biologic events took place during the Jurassic Period. The first was the appearance of the first bird. Known from a feather, two skeletons, and the fragments of a third, this important fossil was collected from a limestone quarry in southern Germany. Named *Archaeopteryx* (which literally means "ancient wing"), this primitive bird still retained certain reptile-like features. For example, its jaws contained teeth and there were claws on its wings. This "early bird" did, nevertheless, have feathers. These clearly identify *Archaeopteryx* as a bird.

The appearance of the mammals was the second great life development of the Jurassic. Known only from fragmental fossil remains, these early mammals appear to have been about the size of a large rat. The structure of their teeth indicates that some of these early creatures were plant-eaters while others ate meat.

England's famous White Chalk Cliffs are typical of rocks of the *Cretaceous Period*. It was here that little Mary Anning made some of her more remarkable fossil discoveries. This is certainly to be expected, for Cretaceous rocks are among the most fossiliferous in the world. Nor is it surprising that the name Cretaceous is derived from the Latin word *creta* meaning chalk. This is certainly a most appropriate name, for Cretaceous rocks typically consist of rather limy or chalky deposits. Typical Cretaceous strata can be seen in the White Cliffs of Dover along the English Channel where these rocks were first studied and described.

During the Cretaceous Period the oceans covered the Atlantic and Gulf Coastal plains of the United States. In addition, a lengthy arm of the sea extended inland from the Gulf of Mexico to the Arctic Ocean, representing the last great submergence of the North American continent.

Plant life of the Early Cretaceous was characterized by ferns, conifers, and cycads. But during Middle Cretaceous time the first *angiosperms*, or flowering plants, appeared. When the period came to a close, Cretaceous plant life closely resembled that of today.

Cretaceous seas were warm and relatively shallow. The fossil record reveals that they contained hosts of invertebrates and many of these have been preserved as fossils. Snails, clams, oysters, and other shellfish were especially numerous, as were the spiny-skinned sea urchins. Particularly notable were the *ammonites*. These coiled cephalopods typically resemble a coiled ram's horn. However, they also assumed other shapes. But despite their great numbers, they were destined for extinction at the end of the Cretaceous Period.

Vertebrate life was represented by a host of fish, amphibians, birds, and primitive mammals. But as in the Triassic and Jurassic Periods, it was the reptiles who held sway over land, sea, and air. There were duck-billed dinosaurs like *Anatosaurus,* horned forms such as *Triceratops,* and tanklike, armored species like *Ankylosaurus.* In addition to these plant-eaters, there were monstrous carnivorous (meat-eating) dinosaurs such as *Tyrannosaurus rex.* Standing some twenty feet tall, *Tyrannosaurus* walked on his hind legs, was forty to fifty feet long and had long dagger-like teeth.

Marine reptiles were common in Cretaceous seas and the still-numerous ichthyosaurs and plesiosaurs were joined by the mosasaurs. Some of these "sea-going lizards" were as much as fifty feet long. They were characterized by a flattened tail, sharp teeth, and four limbs that were modified into paddle-like flippers.

The sea also contained giant turtles. Some species were as much as twelve feet long.

The flying reptiles continued to make remarkable strides during the Cretaceous. Perhaps the best known pterosaur of this time was *Pteranodon*. Although its short, two-foot body weighed only ten or twelve pounds, this peculiar beast had a wingspread of as much as twenty-five feet!

Despite the great success of the reptilian hordes of the Mesozoic, the dinosaurs—along with the flying reptiles and most marine reptiles—became extinct at the end of the Cretaceous Period. The cause of their extinction still remains one of science's greatest mysteries.

Cretaceous climates appear to have been mild and temperate. However, it must have been much colder in Australia, for there is evidence of glaciation there in Early Cretaceous time.

The Laramide Revolution, a great orogeny that produced the Rocky Mountain system, punctuated the end of the Cretaceous Period and along with it the Mesozoic Era. Much folding and faulting accompanied this great mountain-building movement and there is evidence of considerable volcanic activity.

MAMMALS INHERIT THE EARTH

A glance at the Geologic Time Scale shows that we are now living during the *Cenozoic Era*. The word "Cenozoic" literally means "recent-life" and, as the name suggests, the plants and animals of this era are characterized by the presence of large numbers of modern species. Although many types of present-day invertebrates appeared during the Cenozoic Era, the major biologic event was the phenomenal expansion of the mammals. These warm-blooded creatures were so numerous and diverse that the Cenozoic has been called the "Age of Mammals."

Cenozoic time began with the *Tertiary Period*. The Tertiary

Certain marine fossils of the Tertiary bear marked resemblance to species that are living today.

derives its name from an old outdated and abandoned classication of geologic time.

Plants of the Tertiary closely resembled forms that are now living and the forests had a decidedly modern appearance. The expansion of hardwood trees, flowering plants, and grasses were particularly notable and probably furthered the expansion of the mammals.

Shellfish—especially clams, oysters, and snails—were abundant in the sea. However, the ammonites that had been so numerous during the Mesozoic were now extinct.

Birds were common during Tertiary time and resembled many of our modern species. Their fossils are not commonly found, however, for the fragile nature of their bodies normally prevents fossilization. A few species of birds attained very great size and some birds lost the ability—or need—to fly.

The relatively sudden extinction of the dinosaur at the end of the Mesozoic triggered the almost explosive development of the mammals. Horses appeared early in the period and were about the size of a small dog. Certain Tertiary mammals were every

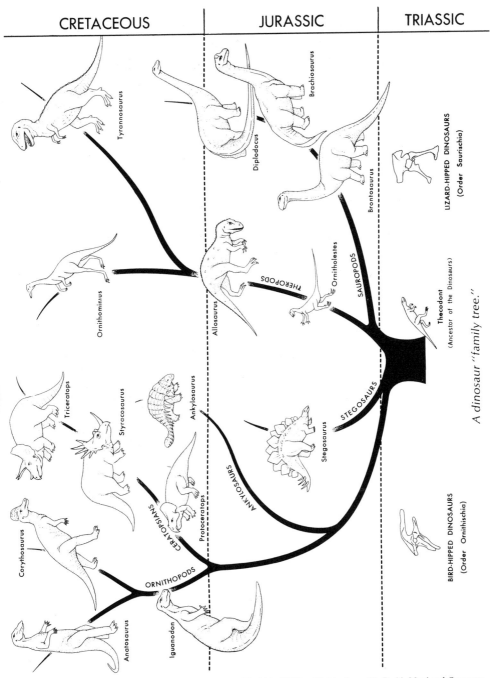

CRETACEOUS   JURASSIC   TRIASSIC

Tyrannosaurus

Brachiosaurus

Diplodocus

Brontosaurus

LIZARD-HIPPED DINOSAURS
(Order Saurischia)

Ornithomimus

Allosaurus

THEROPODS

Ornitholestes

SAUROPODS

Thecodont
(Ancestor of the Dinosaurs)

A dinosaur "family tree."

Triceratops

Styracosaurus

Ankylosaurus

ANKYLOSAURS

Stegosaurus

STEGOSAURS

Corythosaurus

Protoceratops

CERATOPSIANS

ORNITHOPODS

BIRD-HIPPED DINOSAURS
(Order Ornithischia)

Anatosaurus

Iguanodon

Wonders of the Dinosaur World by William H. Matthews III, Dodd, Mead and Company

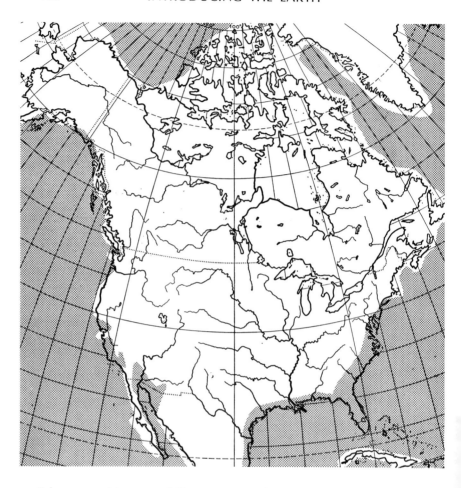

Paleogeographic map of Tertiary time. The margins of the continent were flooded in places; otherwise North America looked much as it does today.

bit as gigantic and bizarre as the reptilian hordes of the Mesozoic. Consider, for example, the uintathere, a great rhinoceros-like beast that weighed many tons and stood as much as seven feet tall at the shoulder! Or, a titanothere such as *Brontotherium* whose elephant-like body and horned skull gave it a most grotesque appearance. Also present were giant pigs and unusual camels and deer.

Tertiary climates appear to have been warm and somewhat humid in North America. But temperatures dropped near the end of the period—a warning of the great sheets of ice that were soon to cover much of North America.

There was considerable crustal unrest in the western United States near the end of Tertiary time. These uplifts continued until the close of the period and were climaxed by the Cascadian Disturbance. This orogeny elevated the Cascade Mountains of Oregon and Washington and the Coast Ranges of California. Much volcanic activity accompanied the mountain-building in the Pacific northwest as revealed by the extensive Columbia River lava flows. In addition, such famous mountains as Mount Shasta and Lassen Peak in California, Mount Hood in Oregon, and Washington's Mount Rainier were all associated with Tertiary volcanic activities.

The *Quaternary Period*, like the Tertiary, got its name from

The monstrous, horned uintathere (left) and the other Tertiary animals are typical of the "Age of Mammals."

Smithsonian Institution

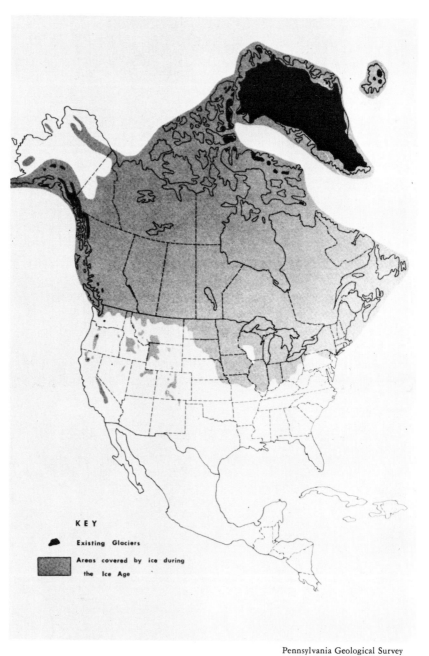

KEY

Existing Glaciers

Areas covered by ice during
the Ice Age

Map of North America during the Ice Age of Quaternary time.

Pennsylvania Geological Survey

The great woolly mammoth was abundant in North America during the Pleistocene glacial epoch.

a rock classification that is no longer in use. The most recent chapter in earth history, this period has been divided into two smaller units of time called the Pleistocene and Holocene (or Recent) Epochs.

Pleistocene time was characterized by great continental glaciers that blanketed much of Canada and the northern United States. Other massive ice sheets rode over parts of Northern Europe and Siberia. At one time during this great Ice Age, approximately one-third of the earth's land surface was buried beneath glacial ice.

The colder temperatures of the Pleistocene had a profound effect on the life of that time. Some forms which had been abundant during the Tertiary could not adjust to the frigid glacial climate and, failing to adapt, they became extinct. But more hardy creatures such as the mastodon, woolly mammoth, musk ox, and woolly rhinoceros adapted to the chilly climate and ranged far and wide.

Restoration of early Pleistocene man drawing on wall of cave.

Among other well-known Pleistocene animals are the saber-toothed cat, giant dire wolf, huge ground sloths, and the thick-shelled glyptodonts. The latter were large armadillo-like mammals which were almost as large as a Volkswagen.

However, the big "news" in Pleistocene time was the appearance of man. Although manlike creatures or near humans developed much earlier, man as we know him today probably appeared some 600,000 years ago. Considering the great age of the earth and how long life has been present on it, man is clearly a relatively new addition to the geologic scene.

The most recent part of the Quaternary Periods is the Holocene, or Recent Epoch. This, the latest chapter in Earth's history, began about 11,000 years ago and continues to this very instant.

Chapter 16

GEOLOGY, ENVIRONMENT, AND MAN

Curious creature that he is, man has always been interested in his surroundings. Fortunately, his curiosity has made him aware of the natural environment and the earth materials at his disposal. He has used caves as protection from the weather, a sharp piece of flint for a knife, iron to shoe his horses, coal for his furnaces, and uranium for energy. From the Stone Age, through the Age of Metals, to the Atomic Age, man has looked to the earth for support. He still does and he always will, for he must.

Nothing on Earth is as important as the earth. Our very lives depend on products derived from weathered rock called soil. Industry relies on Earth's treasure house of mineral resources such as lead, iron, coal, and petroleum. We enjoy the beauty of gem stones and breathtaking scenery produced by geologic processes. Indeed, our bodies consist of some of the same chemicals and minerals that make up the crust of the earth.

Small wonder, then, that man's curiosity about the earth has steadily grown. This increased interest in the earth has come as the result of necessity. And somewhere along the way—about 200 years ago—the science of geology was born.

As the science of geology has matured we have learned to use geologic products and geologic knowledge in many ways. Preceding chapters have reviewed some of the more theoretical or

Geologists are literally working from the ocean floors to the moon to learn more about Earth and our environment.

U. S. Navy

scientific aspects of earth science. In the remaining pages of this book let us briefly consider some of the more practical applications of geology.

One of the geologist's major goals is the exploration, development, and conservation of our nonrenewable mineral resources. These rapidly dwindling, irreplacable materials include metallic minerals such as iron, lead, and gold, and the equally important nonmetallic minerals such as salt and sulfur. The fossil fuels, coal and petroleum, are basic to the above, for they provide the energy needed to convert the raw mineral products into usable goods.

Why "nonrenewable" mineral resources? These natural raw materials are a one-time "crop," for once they are gone they will not grow back. When the coal has been stripped from the ground and sent to the furnace, all that remains is an ugly scar on the landscape. Unlike a fruit tree that will bloom and produce fruit

The never-ending search for oil has led man to drill about five miles
into the earth's crust.

Once the aluminum ore has been stripped from this pit it will not "grow" back. Geologists seek to conserve and find new sources of such nonrenewable mineral resources.

the following season, the coal is gone . . . forever. And so it is with the other minerals that we extract from Earth's crust. The geologist is acutely aware of our shrinking supply of minerals. He also knows that new mineral products will not appear in their place for thousands of years—if ever.

The health of the world's industrial economy depends to a large degree on the availability and utilization of these different kinds of earth materials. Thus the ever-increasing need for more mineral resources—coupled with the expanding world population —have placed growing demands on geology and earth scientists.

Thus far, advanced research techniques and new methods of mineral exploration have enabled the geologist to keep pace with these requirements.

But world needs continue to grow as mineral reserves constantly shrink. Consequently, mineral explorationists are continually looking for new areas to prospect. Within the last few years they have become more and more interested in the ocean floor. If most of our present wealth comes from 29.2 per cent of the exposed continental crust, is it not logical to explore the 70.8 per cent beneath the sea? It would seem so, for more than five billion dollars worth of oil, natural gas, and minerals have already been produced from submerged continental shelves of the United States.

Meanwhile, earth scientists have not confined their interest and activities to the pursuit of mineral wealth. Like any concerned

Soil erosion is a serious environmental problem. Specially trained geologists can help farmers save their precious soil.

Soil Conservation Service, U. S. Department of Agriculture

citizen, the geologist is becoming increasingly alarmed by the mounting—and seemingly insurmountable—problems of man and his physical environment. He, perhaps more than any other scientist, is aware of man's dependency on the earth. And, since Earth is his reason for being, the geologist feels a special sense of commitment to this fragile planet.

To meet the challenge of the environmental crisis, a new type of geologist has appeared. The *environmental geologist*, as he is usually called, is dedicated to the conservation of our mineral resources and the application of geology to human needs. Environmental geologists hope to make public officials, engineers, and home builders aware of geologic hazards in the areas in which homes are to be built. A great deal of earthquake and landslide damage could be avoided if geologic advice is obtained before

Landslides like those plaguing parts of California are usually caused by unstable geologic conditions further aggravated by man.

George Cleveland, California Division of Mines and Geology

The white line marks the approximate location of California's active San Andreas Fault. The surface in this area shifted about five feet during the 1906 earthquake. Environmental geologists would like to help city planners avoid such geologic hazzards.

U. S. Geological Survey.

building in areas that are subject to earthquakes and mass wasting.

In addition to pointing out potential geologic danger areas, the environmental geologist is interested in the proper disposal of waste materials, especially those that are radioactive. The reduction of marine erosion in coastal areas, soil conservation techniques, and pollution related to harmful elements in the soil are but a few of the problems with which this new breed of geologist is concerned. Hopefully, other scientists, conscientious citizens, industry, and government will continue to join the geologist in his fight to save the environment. Then—and only then—will this amazing earth be preserved for the generations that lie ahead.

Glossary

AFTERSHOCK—An earthquake that follows a larger earthquake and originates at or near the focus of the larger quake.

ALPINE GLACIER—A stream of ice occupying a depression in mountainous terrain and moving toward a lower level; also called valley or mountain glacier.

AMBER—The fossilized sticky sap of ancient trees.

AQUIFER—A porous water-bearing rock formation.

ASTEROID—One of many small bodies that revolves around the sun between the orbits of Mars and Jupiter.

ASTHENOSPHERE—The zone of weakness in the upper part of Earth's mantle where plastic movements may occur.

ATMOSPHERE—The air surrounding the earth.

ATOM—The smallest subdivision of an element that has all the properties of that element.

AVALANCHE—A large mass of snow and ice moving rapidly downslope.

BEDROCK—The unweathered solid rock of the earth's crust.

BIOSPHERE—The living realm of the earth's plants and animals.

CALDERA—A great basinlike depression formed by the destruction of a volcanic cone.

CINDER CONE—A steep-sided cone composed primarily of ash and cinders and formed by volcanic action.

COMPOSITE CONE—A volcanic cone composed of alternate layers of lava and cinders.

COMPOUND—A distinct substance formed by the union of two or more elements in definite proportions by weight, such as many minerals.

CONTINENTAL GLACIER—An ice sheet that obscures mountains and plains or a large section of a continent.

CONVECTION CELL—A pair of convection currents adjacent to each other.

COPROLITE—The fossil excrement of animals.

CORE—The heavy, central interior zone of the earth. Also, a section of rock obtained from depth by drilling operations.

COSMOGONY—Speculation on the origin of the universe, including Earth and the solar system.

CRUST—The outer shell of the solid earth surrounding the mantle.

DECOMPOSITION—The chemical decay or breakdown of a rock, known also as chemical weathering.

DEPOSITION—The laying down of material which may later become a rock or mineral deposit.

DISINTEGRATION—The breakdown of a rock by mechanical means, known also as physical weathering or mechanical weathering.

DISSECTED—To be cut into hills and valleys by erosion.

DOME MOUNTAINS—Mountains that form when sedimentary beds are uplifted into broad, circular domes.

ELEMENT—A basic mineral substance that cannot be reduced into another substance except by radioactivity.

EPICENTER—Point on the earth's surface directly above the focus or hypocenter of an earthquake.

EROSIONAL MOUNTAINS—Land forms of high elevation and small summit area formed as a result of erosion.

EXPLOSIVE CONE—See cinder cone.

EXTRUSIVE—As applied to igneous rocks, rocks formed from materials ejected or poured out upon the earth's surface, such as volcanic rocks.

FAULT—A fracture in a rock surface, along which there is displacement of the broken surfaces.

FAULT BLOCK MOUNTAIN—A mountain bounded by one or more faults.

FAULT PLANE—A fracture in the rock along which movement has taken place.

FAULT SCARP—A small cliff formed at the surface along a fault line.

FISSURE—An open fracture in a rock surface.

FISSURE ERUPTION—The extrusion of lava from a fissure, or crack, in the earth's crust.

FOCUS—See epicenter.

FOLDED MOUNTAINS—Mountains formed from folding of the rocks.

FOSSIL—Any remains or traces of plants or animals that have been naturally preserved in deposits of a past geologic age.

FOSSIL FUELS—Organic remains (once living matter) used to produce heat or power by combustion. Includes petroleum, natural gas, and coal.

FOSSILIZATION—The process by which plant and animal remains become fossils.

FUMAROLES—Fissures or holes in volcanic regions, from which steam and other volcanic gases are emitted.

GASTROLITH—Highly polished, well-rounded pebbles found associated with certain reptilian fossils; "stomach stones."

GEOCHRONOLOGY—The study of time in relation to the history of the earth.

GEOLOGIC TIME SCALE—A chronologic sequence of units of earth time.

GEOSYNCLINE—A great elongated downfold in which great thicknesses of sediment accumulate over a long period of time.

GEYSER—A hot spring which erupts periodically, throwing out steam and hot water.

GLACIATION—Major advance of ice sheets over a large part of the earth's surface.

GLACIER—A slowly moving mass of recrystallized ice flowing forward as a result of gravitational attraction.

GLACIOLOGIST—A geologist who specializes in the study of glaciers and their geologic effects.

GLOBAL TECTONICS—See plate tectonics.

GONDWANALAND—Hypothetical continent thought to have broken up in the geologic past. The resulting fragments are postulated to form present-day South America, Africa, Australia, India, and Antarctica.

GROUNDWATER—The underground water beneath the water table, which saturates all pores and openings in the soil and rocks.

HALF-LIFE—The time interval during which half of a given amount of radioactive material disintegrates.

HOT SPRINGS—A spring that brings hot water to the earth's surface.

HYDROLOGIC CYCLE—The continuous process whereby water evaporates from the sea, is precipitated to the land, and eventually moves back to the sea.

HYDROSPHERE—All the water upon the earth's surface or in the open spaces below the surface.

HYPOCENTER—The place in the earth's crust or mantle where an earthquake has occurred.

ICE AGE—The glacial period, or Pleistocene Epoch, of the Quaternary Period.

ICE SHEET—A large moundlike mass of glacier ice spreading in several or all directions from a center.

ICELANDIC ERUPTION—*See* fissure eruption.

IGNEOUS ROCK—Rocks which have solidified from lava or molten rock called magma.

INTENSITY (of an earthquake)—A number related to the effects of earthquake waves on man, structures, and the earth's surface at a given location.

INTERFACE—A surface forming a common boundary between two objects or spheres.

INTRUSIVE (INTRUSION)—Applied to igneous rocks which have been emplaced below the surface.

ISOSTASY—The state of balance of the earth's crust.

ISOTOPES—Elements having the same atomic numbers but differing in atomic weights and some chemical properties.

LANDSLIDE—The relatively rapid movement of large masses of rock and earth down the slope of a hill or mountain.

LAVA—Magma that has poured out onto the surface of the earth, or rock that has solidified from such magma.

LAVA DOME—*See* shield volcano.

LAVA PLATEAU—A broad, elevated, flat-topped highland formed from successive lava flows from fissure eruptions.

LAURASIA—A hypothetical continent thought to have broken up in the geologic past to form Eurasia and North America.

LIGHT YEAR—The distance that light travels in one year.

LITHOSPHERE—The entire solid part of the earth (crust, mantle, core).

LONG WAVES—Earthquake surface waves, also called L waves.

MAGMA—Molten rock material beneath the earth's surface and from which igneous rocks are formed.

MAGMA RESERVOIR—Subterranean chambers containing molten rock called magma.

MAGNITUDE (of an earthquake)—A number related to the total energy released by an earthquake.

MANTLE—The thick dense part of the lithosphere beneath the crust and to a depth of about 1800 miles below the surface.

MANTLE ROCK—A layer of loose soil, earth, or rock which covers bedrock.

MARINE—Belonging to, or originating in, the sea.

MASS MOVEMENT—Surface movements of earth materials caused primarily by gravity.

MASS WASTING—Erosional processes caused chiefly by gravity.

METAMORPHIC ROCK—Rock that has been changed from its original state by heat, pressure, chemical action, or some combination of these factors.

METAMORPHISM—Extensive change of rocks or minerals due to extreme heat and pressure within the earth.

METEORIC WATER—Ground water derived primarily from precipitation.

MICROFOSSIL—Fossils of microscopic size, not readily visible or studied without the aid of a microscope.

MILKY WAY—The galaxy to which the earth belongs.

MINERAL—A naturally occurring inorganic substance possessing definite chemical and physical properties.

MINERALOGIST—A geologist who specializes in studying minerals.

MODIFIED MERCALLI ITENSITY SCALE—A scale designed to express the effect of earthquake waves on man, structures, or the earth's surface at any given place.

MOHO—*See* Mohorovičić Discontinuity.

MOHOROVIČIĆ DISCONTINUITY—The zone of contact between the crust and the mantle.

MUDFLOW—The movement of a large mass of mud and rock debris down a valley as a result of heavy rains.

NUNATAK—A mountaintop projecting above an ice sheet, as in Greenland.

OCEANIC RIDGES—A belt of submarine mountains rising from the ocean floors and located nearly midway between the continents.

PALEOGEOGRAPHIC MAP—A map showing possible distribution of ancient seas and landmasses.

PALEOMAGNETISM—The condition of Earth's magnetic field as it has existed through geologic time.

PANGEA—A hypothetical continent from which present continents were derived as a result of fragmentation and drifting.

PETROGRAPHER—A geologist who specializes in the description and classification of rocks.

PLANET—A heavenly body such as the Earth, having no light of its own and revolving in an orbit about a star.

PLATE TECTONICS—The concept that assumes presence of drifting crustal plates that have shifted to form continents and folded mountains.

PLUTONIC—Applied to rocks which have formed at great depths below the surface.

PRECESSION—The slight wobbling motion of the earth as it moves on its axis.

PROTOPLANET—An enlargement in the gaseous envelopes in space surrounding the sun; primitive planet.

PROTOSUN—The original mass of solar material from which the sun may have formed.

PUMICE—Surface lava which looks like foam and hardens into a spongy rock.

PYROCLASTIC—A fragmental rock formed of rock fragments thrown out of volcanoes; for example, cinders, volcanic bombs, etc.

RADIOMETRIC DATING—The use of radioactive material such as uranium or Carbon-14 to obtain absolute age of an object.

RICHTER SCALE—A scale designed to express earthquake magnitude, or the measure of energy released by an earthquake.

RIFT—A large fracture in the earth's crust as in the mid-ocean ridges.

ROCK-FORMING MINERALS—Common minerals which compose large percentages of the rocks of the lithosphere.

RUNOFF—The water which flows on the ground surface, tending to drain through streams toward the sea.

SEDIMENT—Rock fragments that have been deposited by settling from a transportation agent such as water, ice, or air.

SEDIMENTARY ROCK—Rocks formed by the accumulation of sediments.

SEICHE—Earthquake-induced periodic oscillation of a body of water.

SEISMIC—Pertaining to, or produced by, earthquakes.

SEISMIC BELTS—Zones of weakness in the earth's crust where frequent earthquake activity occurs.

SEISMIC SEA WAVE—See tsunami.

SEISMIC WAVES—Earthquake waves.

SEISMOGRAM—The graphic record of earthquake waves that indicates the time, length, distance, direction, and intensity of an earthquake.

SEISMOGRAPH—An instrument which detects and records earthquake waves.

SEISMOLOGIST—One who studies and interprets the effects of earthquake activity.

SEISMOLOGY—The scientific study of earthquakes and other earth tremors.

SHIELD VOLCANO—A volcano composed almost exclusively of lava; known also as shield cone, lava dome, or volcanic shield.

SILICATES—Rock-forming minerals containing the elements silicon and oxygen.

SOIL CREEP—Slow movement of a mass of soil down a slope, caused by the soil's own weight.

SOLAR SYSTEM—The heavenly unit consisting of the sun, planets, planetoids, moons, comets, and meteors.

STRATA—Rock layers or beds.

STRATIFIED ROCKS—Sedimentary rocks; those formed in beds, layers, or strata.

STRATOVOLCANO—Volcano having a cone of alternate layers of lava and solid fragments; also called composite cone.

TEMBLOR—An earthquake.

TERRESTRIAL—Belonging to or originating on the land.

TEXTURE—The physical appearance of a rock as indicated by the size, shape, and arrangement of the materials comprising the rock.

TILTMETER—A device used to measure doming up of a volcano from pressure of underlying lava.

TRANSFORM FAULTS—A lateral or sideways rock displacement such as along the oceanic ridges.

TRANSPIRATION—The process by which living plants release water vapor to the atmosphere.

TRANSVERSE—At right angles to length.

TSUNAMI—A giant seismic sea wave generated by submarine earthquakes or other disturbances on the sea floor, sometimes incorrectly called "tidal wave."

UNCONFORMITY—An eroded bedrock area covered by younger sedimentary rocks and representing a break in the geologic record.

UNIFORMITARIANISM, PRINCIPLE OF—The doctrine of "the present is the key to the past"; that geologic history is best interpreted in the light of what is known about the present.

VALLEY GLACIER—*See* alpine glacier.

VOLCANIC—Pertaining to volcanoes or any rocks associated with volcanic activity at or below the surface.

VOLCANISM—A general term including all types of activity due to movement of magma.

VOLCANO—An opening or vent in the earth's crust through which volcanic materials are erupted; refers also to the land form developed by the accumulation of volcanic materials around the vent.

VOLCANOLOGIST—One who studies and interprets volcanoes and their related phenomena.

WEATHERING—The natural physical and chemical breakdown of rocks under atmospheric conditions.

For Further Reading

Hopefully, this introduction to the earth will encourage the reader to want to know more about geology and our planet. There are many excellent books on this subject and only a few of these can be listed here.

Ames, Gerald and Wyler, Rose. *Earth's Story*. Mankato, Minnesota: Creative Educational Society, 1962.

Beiser, Arthur and The Editors of Life. *The Earth*. New York: Time, Inc., 1963.

Branley, Franklyn M. *The Earth: Planet Number Three*. New York: Thomas Y. Crowell Company, 1966.

Brown, Billye and Brown, Walter R. *Historical Catastrophes: Volcanoes*. Reading, Massachusetts: Addison-Wesley Publishing Company, 1970.

Bullard, Fred M. *Volcanoes: In History, In Theory, In Eruption*. Austin: University of Texas Press, 1962.

Carlisle, Norman. *Riches of the Sea: The New Science of Oceanology*. New York: Sterling Publishing Company, 1967; London: J. M. Dent, 1968.

Clayton, Keith. *The Crust of the Earth: The Story of Geology*. Garden City, New York: The Natural History Press, 1967.

Colbert, Edwin H. *The Dinosaur Book*, 2nd Edition. New York: McGraw-Hill Book Company, 1951.

Farb, Peter. *The Story of Life*. Irvington-on-Hudson, New York: Harvey House, Inc., 1962.

Fenton, Carroll L. and Mildred A. *The Fossil Book*. New York: Doubleday & Company, Inc., 1965.

——————. *The Rock Book*. New York: Doubleday & Company, Inc., 1940.

Fenton, Carroll Lane. *Tales Told by Fossils*. New York: Doubleday & Company, Inc., 1966.

Herbert, Don and Bardossi, Fulvio. *Kilauea: Case History of a Volcano*. New York: Harper & Row, 1968.

Holden, Raymond P. *Famous Fossil Finds*. New York: Dodd, Mead & Company, 1966.

Hotton, Nicholas, III. *Dinosaurs*. New York: Pyramid Publications, 1963.

Lauber, Patricia. *All About the Planet Earth*. New York: Random House, 1962.

Matthews, William H., III. *Fossils: An Introduction to Prehistoric Life*. New York: Barnes & Noble, 1962.

_____. *Invitation to Geology: The Earth Through Time and Space*. New York: The Natural History Press and Doubleday & Company, 1971.

_____*Science Probes the Earth: New Frontiers of Geology*. New York: Sterling Publishing Company, 1969.

_____. *Soils*. New York: Franklin Watts, Inc., 1970.

_____*The Story of the Earth*. Irvington-on-Hudson, New York: Harvey House, Inc., 1968.

_____. *The Story of Volcanoes and Earthquakes*. Irvington-on-Hudson, New York: Harvey House, Inc., 1969.

_____. *Wonders of the Dinosaur World*. New York: Dodd, Mead & Company, 1963.

Page, Lou W. *The Earth and Its Story*. Columbus, Ohio: American Education Publications, 1961.

Pearl, Richard M. *Rocks and Minerals*. New York: Barnes & Noble, 1956.

_____. *Wonders of Rocks and Minerals*. New York: Dodd, Mead & Company, 1961.

Pough, Frederick H. *All About Volcanoes and Earthquakes*. New York: Random House, 1953.

Roberts, Elliott. *Our Quaking Earth*. Boston: Little, Brown and Company, 1963.

Sterling, Dorothy. *The Story of Caves*. Garden City, New York: Doubleday & Company, Inc., 1956.

Strahler, Arthur N. *The Story of Our Earth*. New York: Home Library Press, 1963.

Thorarinsson, Sigurdur. *Surtsey: The New Island in the North Atlantic*. New York, The Viking Press, 1967.

Vaughan-Jackson, Genevieve. *Mountains of Fire: An Introduction to the Science of Volcanoes*. New York: Hastings House, Publishers, Inc., 1962.

Wilcoxson, Kent H. *Chains of Fire: The Story of Volcanoes*. Philadelphia: Chilton Books, 1966.

Wyckoff, Jerome. *Geology: Our Changing Earth Through the Ages*. New York: Golden Press, 1967.

Yasso, Warren E. *Oceanography: A Study of Inner Space*. New York: Holt, Rinehart and Winston, Inc., 1965.

Zim, Herbert S. and Shaffer, Paul R. *Rocks and Minerals*. New York: Golden Press, 1957.

Index

ABOUT THE AUTHOR

WILLIAM H. MATTHEWS III is Professor of Geology at Lamar University, Beaumont, Texas. He received his B.A. and M.A. degrees from Texas Christian University, and is listed in *American Men of Science* and *Who's Who in American Education*.

Prominent in numerous scientific and educational organizations, he is past president of the National Association of Geology Teachers, and is Visiting Geoscientist for the American Geological Institute in Washington and for the Texas Academy of Science.

In addition to articles in scientific and professional journals, Professor Matthews is the author of over two dozen books in the fields of geology and paleontology. He is perhaps best known for his adult work, *Fossils: An Introduction to Prehistoric Life*, but his thorough knowledge and lively writing style have made his titles for young readers—about dinosaurs, volcanoes, and other aspects of earth science—unusually interesting ones.

D